WHO SAYS RETIREMENT HAS TO BE BORING?

Regina Kessler

PHAROS BOOKS
A SCRIPPS HOWARD COMPANY
NEW YORK

Pharos Books are available at special discounts on bulk purchases
for sales promotions, premiums, fundraising or educational use.
For details, contact:
Special Sales Department
Pharos Books
200 Park Avenue
New York, NY 10166

First published in 1991.

Library of Congress Cataloging-in-Publication Data:
Kessler, Regina.
Who says retirement has to be boring? / Regina Kessler.
p.   cm.
Includes index.
ISBN 0-88687-531-5 : $15.95
1. Retirement—United States—Planning.   2. Retirees—United
States—Psychology.   I. Title.
HQ1063.2.K47   1991
646.7′9—dc20   91-19598   CIP

Printed in the United States of America

Pharos Books
A Scripps Howard Company
200 Park Avenue
New York, N.Y. 10166

10 9 8 7 6 5 4 3 2 1

WHO SAYS RETIREMENT HAS TO BE BORING?

To my brother Jeffrey
who eased the way

Grow old along with me!
The best is yet to be,
The last of life, for which the first was made.

ROBERT BROWNING

Contents

Acknowledgments

I wish to thank my teachers Dr. Scout Lee Gunn, Dr. Carol Ann Peterson, and Dr. Jean Mundy for their inspiration and pioneering work in the field of leisure education; my brother Jeffrey for his expert instruction and lifelong support; Clinton Reeves and Shelley Conger for their assistance in preparing the manuscript, Derick Simmons for getting me back up whenever my computer went down; my agent Ethan Ellenberg and my editor Sharilyn Jee for believing in my project; and, Kintana and Merlin for keeping me company and lowering my blood pressure during the long hours of work. I also want to thank the NCOA, AARP and all the people and organizations who freely shared information with me and the New York Public Library system for providing access to research materials.

CHAPTER I

The Gift of Time: Redefining Your Goals

⋙

"Would you tell me, please, which way I ought to go from here?"

"That depends a great deal on where you want to get to," said the cat.

LEWIS CARROLL
Alice in Wonderland

Eleven-thirty was really too early for lunch, but Harry was busy heating up last night's dinner anyhow. Preparing food made him feel useful. At least he was doing something productive, even if it was only taking yesterday's stew out of the refrigerator and putting it on the stove.

Early lunch has become a ritual for him since he retired. It helped break up the day. He usually watched "My Three Sons" while he ate. He didn't really like the show but it wasn't bad company. The story line was so thin he could easily follow it between bites. He liked to finish eating and have all the dishes cleaned and put away before "As the World Turns." Sometimes he saved his dessert for "General Hospital," the soap opera that was the highlight of his afternoon.

Then it was time for the martini. He figured one martini was OK. In the old days he would have had three by now. Ethel usually called about 1:15. The conversation was always the same.

"Hi dear, how are you doing? Just called to say hello. Would you pick up a cake at Davis Bakery? Oh, and put the chicken in at about five o'clock. Don't set it at 400 degrees like you did the last time. Remember, 350 degrees. Well, I've got to get back to work. Have a good day. See you later."

He never told Ethel about the martinis or the soap operas. He didn't have to. Forty years of service to the same company surely earned him the right to spend his time as he chose. He hadn't expected *this,* though. Somehow, he had thought retirement would be different, although now he wasn't sure exactly what he thought it was going to be like.

Actually, he hadn't thought much about it at all. Of course he checked into his pension benefits a few months before his retirement date. When people asked about his plans, he told them he was going to buy a camper, fill the back with the pipes he had once sold to earn a living, and travel around the country, stopping where he wanted for as long as he wanted. When he needed a little cash, he would call on some old customers and sell them some pipes. He had picked up a few brochures on campers and bought himself a red plaid hunting jacket. That was the only thought he gave to the whole thing, until one day he didn't have to catch the 8:05.

Now he knew traveling across country in his camper was only a fantasy, at least as long as Ethel was working. He couldn't understand why she continued to work. It made him angry. For the first time in his life, he felt vaguely dependent on Ethel. Not that he couldn't still take care of them. His pension paid their basic expenses. But without Ethel's salary, they really couldn't afford their little luxuries, like their annual trip to their daughter's house or the expensive presents they bought the grandchildren.

What was he going to do with the rest of the afternoon? He could reorganize the kitchen. It seemed to him that Ethel's system was very illogical. He rearranged the utensils according to how frequently they were used. Then he put the spices in alphabetical order. This project so absorbed him that he almost forgot to put the chicken in the oven. Then he remembered the cake. He was halfway out the door before he realized he was still in his pajamas.

Ethel was home before Harry arrived with the cake. She was furious. She had said nothing when Harry insisted that she submit monthly purchase orders for cleanser, dish soap, and cat food. Buying by the case seemed weird to her, but she let it go. She didn't even quibble when Harry plotted their toilet paper use on a graph or did a yearly schedule of household chores, complete with goals and objectives. But now he had gone too far. He had invaded her kitchen.

Harry was hurt. He thought Ethel was being unreasonable. He was only trying to run the household more efficiently— and keep from losing his mind.

Harry's predicament is a common one. The kids are grown. The mortgage is paid off. You don't have to go to work anymore. Now what are you going to do?

Everyone has some sort of retirement plan. Most people dream about the day they can sleep till noon, leave work clothes on the hanger or in the drawer, and spend the day as they please. But after an initial honeymoon period, the reality of unlimited leisure becomes the real challenge of retirement. Those who fail to adjust to unstructured, unlimited time become bored, depressed, and aimless. Those who take advantage of the opportunities leisure offers, however, make retirement the best time of their lives.

Underestimating the impact of leisure is the biggest mistake pre-retirees make. They put their finances in order and assume everything is ready. But the kind of leisure today's retirees face is a new phenomenon: past generations could only expect to live a few good years beyond retirement. Due to medical advances, health consciousness, and early retirement, however, you can look forward to fifteen to twenty healthy, active years—one quarter of your life—to spend in leisure.

You are part of a newly emerging leisure class composed of more than 25 million retired people and growing larger each day as another five thousand Americans reach their sixty-fifth birthdays. Unlike any leisure class known to history, you were not born to leisure. Work formed the fabric and backbone of your life. Work gave your life structure and meaning. Adjusting to leisure after a lifetime of work takes more than finding the right hobby. You'll have to develop new attitudes, skills, and values if retirement is to be the pleasant experience you deserve.

Though you spent years preparing for work, you've probably given little thought to planning for leisure. Up until now, most pre-retirement counseling and advice focused on financial preparation. Financial security is certainly essential for a comfortable retirement, but contentment is not guaranteed by any income level. In studying pre-retirees, Dr. Daniel Ogilvie of Rutgers University discovered that the strongest factor in life satisfaction is how much time a person spends doing the things he does best, enjoys the most, and finds the most meaningful. "Much of the pre-retirement counseling going on in corporations these days has finances as the primary focus," says Dr. Ogilvie (*New York Times,* December 29, 1986).

It is, of course, important to know about pensions and diversification of assets, Social Security benefits, and the like, but people might also want to know that for middle-income groups, income accounts for a trivial degree of people's satisfaction with their lives after retirement.

The best way to prevent the negative aspects associated with aging such as debilitation, loss of vigor, loneliness, and exclusion from the mainstream of society is to remain active and pursue specific interests. Dr. Robert Weiss, dean emeritus of Columbia University's School of Public Health and author of *The Complete Guide to Health and Wellness after 50*, says, "I think it's terribly important to retire in terms of what you yourself enjoy and feel are the necessary returns you want to get out of life." Denise Loftus, manager of work force education at the American Association of Retired People, states,

> Lots of people think that financial planning is all there is to it and I just want to make the point that retirement planning should be so much broader. I think that if you would talk to people who have retired, they would confirm that the financial side is critical, but even if you had all the money in the world, if you don't know what you're going to do and you don't have something meaningful to occupy the hours that used to be work, you won't be happy.

One leading pre-retirement consulting firm, Retirement Advisors, asked retirees what advice they have for those preparing to retire. While financial planning was at the top of the list, cited by 25 percent of those responding, 24 percent, a close second, stressed developing interests that keep one involved.

The problems retirees face in dealing with leisure are a well kept secret. Soon after retirement, retirees generally lose contact with their fellow workers. On the rare occasions they are seen, such as at the annual Christmas party or awards dinner, they look cheerful and sporty, perpetuating the myth that retirement is one continuous holiday. But anyone who has ever been out of work for an extended period of time knows that leisure is a very different matter when it is the only time one has.

Your entire sense of time changes. Though your built-in

clock wakes you at the usual hour, there is no need to dress or be anywhere in particular. Weekends are indistinguishable from weekdays. Having the tennis court or library to yourself is great, but relaxing while everyone else is working can provoke guilt. Scheduling can become a problem. After so many years of being occupied between nine and five from Monday to Friday, it's difficult to figure out when to do anything. Tasks that were always done on time may be neglected because you think, "Oh, I don't have to do that today." You may feel disoriented, out of sync with the rest of the world.

Even lunch can become a problem, too. At work lunch is a welcome break; a time to get together with friends or to relax. It can also be an exciting time, a chance to button down a contract or launch a new project. Now, like Harry, you may find yourself alone, heating up last night's dinner and watching the soaps.

Feelings of loneliness and isolation are common in retirement. Separation from the interactions of the workplace result in a void that must be filled with activities providing opportunities for socialization. Otherwise, you may end up relating only to family members or a small circle of friends as opposed to the many different kinds of people you came in contact with at work.

Perhaps most difficult of all is adjusting to the loss of a professional identity. Our work role is so strong a part of our sense of self that losing it feels like losing ourselves. Though we play many roles in life, it is our work role that most often defines us. When we meet someone for the first time, we tell them what we do for a living as if that sums up who we are. But in retirement, the other roles we play become more prominent; our work role dissolves. Success can no longer be measured in terms of a pay check or job status, and feelings of self-worth must come from other sources. We underestimate the many satisfactions we get from work, thinking that money is the main reward. But work fulfills a gamut of needs. It provides a sense of direction, importance, purpose, and structure. The need for recognition, accomplishment, and productivity do not disappear the day you retire. They must be met in new ways.

Adjusting to leisure after a lifetime of work requires a fundamental change in the value system by which you have lived. The basic concepts that motivated your actions no longer apply. Working hard won't get you ahead. Your earning capacity has reached its peak. There are no more raises, promotions, or titles to strive for. You don't need a big house or two cars and the kids' tuition has long been paid.

Coming from a work-oriented background, you may only be able to conceive of leisure in terms of work; the time away from work, a reward for work well done, or time to refresh yourself for more work. Subconsciously you may even harbor disdain for leisure, having heard many negative messages about it in your childhood. "Idle hands are the work of the devil." "Play is for kids." "Don't spend money on foolishness." If you still equate leisure with idleness, you may fear retirement, assuming you will no longer be useful.

The work ethic we inherited from our founding fathers served us well when all hands were needed to clear and till the soil, and everyone worked until his or her last ounce of strength was spent. But in a new age, where leisure belongs to many of our most experienced citizens, this orientation limits our potential. The ancient Greeks developed a strong *leisure* ethic. They believed that the purpose of work was to obtain leisure and that happiness was only possible in leisure. The contributions they made to culture in the form of drama, art, philosophy, music, literature, and architecture prove that, for them, leisure was far from idleness. To find a concept of leisure that would serve us well today, we need only turn to Aristotle. He believed that leisure is a state of being in which one is free to do what one wants for its own sake and its own end.

Now that you are free to do what you want for no other reason than you want to do it, what will you do?

EVALUATING YOUR ATTITUDE TOWARD LEISURE

After years of conforming to schedules and structures imposed on you from the outside, you must now set your own goals and determine your own priorities. It is time to catch your breath, reflect on what is truly important to you, and expend your energies on what brings you the most joy. If early in life you put aside your best skills and deepest interests because of obligations and responsibilities, you can now rediscover them and develop your unique talents. You can start all over again. This time do things the way you want, and in your own good time.

Before exploring the opportunities presented in the following chapters, take some time to examine your interests and attitudes. This leisure-evaluation system* is designed to help you

- reevaluate and redefine your concept of leisure
- determine what is truly important to you, and
- devise a plan for a satisfying retirement.

You will learn where your time really goes, what your true interests are, what bores you, what makes you happy, what keeps you from enjoying more. You'll discover what you'll miss about work and what you won't. You'll find that your occupation is only one aspect of who you are and that you have only begun to explore your potential.

You've worked hard for the good things in life. Begin enjoying them now!

* Many of these exercises are based on the work of Sidney B. Simon, Leland W. Howe, Howard Kirschenbaum in *Values Clarification* (New York, NY: Hart Publishing, 1972) and Chester F. McDowell, Jr., in *Leisure Counseling: Selected Lifestyle Processes* (Eugene, OR: University of Oregon, 1976).

HOW MUCH LEISURE TIME DO YOU HAVE?

Leisure time doesn't mean time to cook dinner or to do chores. It means time in which you are free to choose what you want to do. To determine how much free time you have, estimate how long you spend on the following obligations and subtract from twenty-four.

	Work Day	Weekend	Retirement
Paid Work	_____	_____	_____
Transportation time	_____	_____	_____
Sleeping	_____	_____	_____
Eating (Include preparation time and clean-up.)	_____	_____	_____
Self Care (ie: shaving, brushing teeth, etc.)	_____	_____	_____
Housework (Chores)	_____	_____	_____
Other Obligations (Include walking the dog, attending meetings, visiting your mother-in-law.)	_____	_____	_____
Total	_____	_____	_____

	Work Day	Weekend	Retirement
	24	24	24
Subtract total from above	− _____	− _____	− _____
Available leisure time	_____	_____	_____

HOW DO YOU SPEND YOUR TIME?

Another way to determine how much time you have for leisure is to take an inventory of where your time goes. You may choose to keep a diary of your time for a week or a month. Use the following chart to compare how you might spend your time during an average work day, weekend, and retirement day.

	Work day	*Weekend*	*Retirement*
5 AM			
6 AM			
7 AM			
8 AM			
9 AM			
10 AM			
11 AM			
12 AM			
1 PM			
2 PM			
3 PM			
4 PM			
5 PM			
6 PM			
7 PM			
8 PM			
9 PM			
10 PM			
11 PM			
12 PM			
1 AM			
2 AM			
3 AM			
4 AM			

WHAT IS LEISURE TO YOU?

Having time free from obligations is essential for leisure, but free time is not necessarily leisure. It is possible to have a leisure experience in the amount of time it takes to smell a rose or spend three weeks on vacation and not experience one moment of it. What is leisure to one person may be work to another and vice versa. To learn more about what leisure is to you, finish the following sentences.

The last time I really had a good time was when _____

_____.

If I could do whatever I wanted I would _____

_____.

When I was a kid, the thing I liked to do best was _____

_____.

I always wanted to _____

_____.

The best time I ever had was _____

_____.

The most playful person I know is _____
because _____.

On rainy days, I _____

_____.

If I had a million dollars I would _____

_____.

To be truly happy, a person needs _____

_____.

Though I've always wanted to, I've been afraid to try _____

_____.

The thing that bores me the most is _____

_____.

I am happiest when _____

_____.

If money and obligations had not been considerations, I would have

_____

_____.

A perfect retirement would include _____

_____

_____

_____

_____.

WHAT DO YOU LIKE TO DO?

Make a list of twenty things you enjoy doing. You don't have to limit yourself to things you actually do. They can be things you used to enjoy doing but haven't done for a long time, or things you always wanted to do but never got around to. They can be silly or serious, as long as the activities bring you pleasure.

	A	P	F	M	C	U	R	$	D	W
1										
2										
3										
4										
5										
6										
7										
8										
9										
10										
11										
12										
13										
14										
15										
16										
17										
18										
19										
20										

Now,

1. Check box A for each activity you enjoy doing alone.
2. Check box P for each activity you enjoy doing with others.
3. Check box F for each activity that contributes to your physical fitness.
4. Check box M for each activity you consider mentally stimulating.
5. Check box C for each activity that provides an outlet for creativity.
6. Check box U for each activity that gives you a feeling of accomplishment and usefulness.
7. Check box R for each activity that relaxes you.
8. Check box $ for each activity that costs more than $10.00 each time you do it.
9. In the box marked D, note the date you last did this activity.
10. Check box W for each activity associated with your former workplace.

You can learn a lot about your leisure preferences by analyzing this list and looking at the boxes you've checked off. Do any patterns emerge? Ask yourself:

What characteristics are shared by most of my favorite activities?
_____.

What characteristics are largely absent from my list of favorite activities?_____
_____.

What kind of activities do I need for a satisfying retirement?_____
_____.

Keep in mind that, in retirement, you need a variety of leisure-time interests to fulfill the many needs you have. These needs may not be the same as when your job filled some of your needs. Where you once craved rest and relaxation, you may now desire challenge and stimulation. What changes might you need to make in your choice of leisure activities to enjoy your retirement more?

WHAT WILL YOU MISS ABOUT WORK?

When people think about retiring, they like to focus on all the things about work they won't miss, like having to keep a schedule or answer to a boss. But what about the things you *will* miss? Work provides lots of satisfaction besides a steady income, including being with other people, working toward a goal, outwitting the competition. After years of active involvement in the work world, you don't suddenly lose interest in challenge or commitment just because you've retired. If you know what kind of satisfaction you receive from work, you will be able to select retirement activities that replace these needs.

On one side of the page, list all of the things you like about work. On the other side, list as many activities as you can think of that may provide similar satisfactions. For example, if one of the things you listed on the left side was challenge, on the right side you might list skiing, crossword puzzles, raising money for cancer research, running the marathon, paneling the den, learning French, etc.

What I Like about Work   *Leisure Substitutes*

_____   _____

_____   _____

_____   _____

_____   _____

_____   _____

_____   _____

_____   _____

_____   _____

_____   _____

_____   _____

_____   _____

_____   _____

WHAT ARE YOUR LEISURE VALUES?

Another way to look at your leisure preferences is to focus on the rewards you get from the experience rather than on the activities themselves. When you know what you want out of your leisure, you can expand your activities and alter your choices to better meet your needs.

Rank the following leisure values in order of importance to you:

_____ *Creative expression*

_____ *Adventure*

_____ *Stimulation*

_____ *Challenge*

_____ *Appreciation of beauty*

_____ *Sense of accomplishment*

_____ *Relaxation*

_____ *Socialization*

_____ *Self-improvement*

_____ *Love of nature*

_____ *Helping others*

_____ *Recognition*

_____ *Physical fitness*

_____ *Spiritual improvement*

_____ *Competition*

_____ *Excitement*

WHAT ARE YOUR LEISURE ATTITUDES?
A PLAYFUL QUIZ

Most of our attitudes toward play and leisure were formed early in life and accepted without examination. Unfortunately, many of these attitudes inhibit our natural playfulness. Such messages as "Don't be a sissy," "Don't be silly," "Don't act like a tomboy," "If you're going to do that, you must do it right," "Good children are clean, quiet, and well behaved," shaped our concepts.

What messages did you receive about play when you were a child? What was your mother's attitude toward play? Your father's? How did your family have fun together? What did your teachers, ministers/ rabbis, and friends think about having fun? What did you tell your children about play? What do you tell your grandchildren?

The following quiz will help you explore your hidden attitudes toward leisure. Circle the letter that most accurately applies.

1. The advice I most frequently hear myself giving to kids about play is:
   A. After you finish your homework, you can go out and play.
   B. Have a good time but don't hurt yourself.
   C. Be sure to put on your play clothes first.

2. On vacation, I prefer to:
   A. See all the sights in the guidebook.
   B. Lie on the beach and relax.
   C. Clean out the closets.
   D. Both A and B.

3. I would define leisure as:
   A. Freedom to do what I choose.
   B. Time to refresh myself for work.
   C. The reward I get for work well done.

4. Anything worth doing is worth doing well.
   A. Agree
   B. Disagree

5. All work and no play makes Jack a dull boy.
   A. Agree
   B. Disagree

6. A family that plays together stays together.
   A. Agree
   B. Disagree

7. List your five favorite leisure activities.
   1.
   2.
   3.
   4.
   5.

Answers

Question 1

A Definitely a work-oriented, non-playful attitude.   (1 point)
B Not bad, but a preoccupation with safety can inhibit
   playfulness.   (3 points)
C Very leisure-oriented instruction. How can kids have fun
   if they are worried about spoiling their clothes?   (5 points)

Question 2

A You're the kind of person who wants to get the most out of
   everything. Be careful. Your perfectionism could make it difficult
   for you to relax.   (3 points)
B You are a person who knows how to relax!   (4 points)
C Uh oh! Possible indication of acute workaholism.   (0 points)
D Variety is the spice of life.   (5 points)

Question 3

A You got it!

B If you value leisure only for its ability to help you work, you are restricting yourself from experiencing your full potential. (0 points)

C You do value leisure, but only if you've paid your dues. (3 points)

Question 4

A This attitude may be helpful at work, but in leisure it can be extremely inhibiting. (You don't have to be Joe DiMaggio to play baseball.) (1 point)

B Great! You're probably not afraid to try something new even if you're lousy at it at first. (5 points)

Question 5

A It sure does. (5 points)

B Watch out. *You* may be dull, dull, dull. (0 points)

Question 6

A Careful, you may be compromising what you like to do in your free time to please others. (1 point)

B You are not afraid to do your own thing. (5 points)

Question 7

Give yourself 2 points for each activity you have participated in during the past four weeks.

Scoring

40–32   Boy, you sure know how to have a good time!

31–15   You have your serious side, but lurking within is a playful person.

Below 15 You may be suffering from serious workaholism, but the fact that you're reading this shows you are ready to change. Keep reading.

WHAT ROLES DO YOU PLAY?

Though we all play many roles in life, we tend to define ourselves in terms of our work role. But we all know we are much more than our occupation and that what we do after work is probably more indicative of who we are. Take a few minutes to list all the roles you play in life. Your list might include such roles as parent, spouse, pet owner, commuter, church member, gardener, committee member, and taxpayer.

Go over your list and cross off all the roles that disappear when you retire. You'll probably find that most of the roles remain. In retirement, these are the roles that are of greatest importance. What are you currently doing to develop these roles? What would you like to do to enhance or improve what you bring to these roles? What other roles would you like to add?

WHAT BRINGS YOU THE MOST JOY?

If you could only choose ten people or things to keep you occupied during your retirement, who or what would you choose?

1. _____
2. _____
3. _____
4. _____
5. _____
6. _____
7. _____
8. _____
9. _____
10. _____

What if you could only choose five? Cross out those you would be willing to leave.

What if you could only choose two? Cross out three more.

What if you could only choose one? What would you be left with?

How much time, energy, and attention do you currently devote to this last remaining person or thing?

RETIREMENT TESTIMONIAL

Imagine you are writing your own retirement testimonial. How would you sum up your career?

The time has come to honor _____ as he/she ends his/her illustrious _____ year career as a _____ . He/she started as a _____ and later went on to _____ . The greatest achievement of his/her career was _____ . Nonetheless, he/she would have liked _____ . He/she will be best remembered for _____ . He/she takes with him/her _____ and leaves behind _____ . Now that he/she is gone, the company will _____ .

STARTING OVER

If I had it to do all over again, I would _____

_____

_____

_____

_____

_____

_____

_____

_____

_____

_____

_____

_____

_____

_____

_____

_____

LEISURE STRATEGIES

The opportunities available to the retired person are unlimited. This book can only touch on some of the possibilities. Many people return to something they enjoyed as a child or devote more time to activities they formerly could only do in their time off. Retirement is also a great chance to explore new options. You can go back to school, use what you know to help others, turn your hobby into a full-time occupation, or do all of these things. Remember, you will need a variety of activities to meet a variety of needs, including the need to do nothing.

Don't limit yourself to what you've always done or to what others think you should do. Only you know what you enjoy. Don't be afraid to try something new even if you make a jerk out of yourself at first. Refusing to do things we don't do *perfectly* is one of the worst ways we limit ourselves. If we don't allow ourselves to feel awkward or make mistakes, we never learn anything. Ask skiers about their first day on skis. If they're honest, they'll tell you how uncomfortable the equipment felt, how scared they were to get on the chair lift, to get off the chair lift, to start that first run. Then they'll tell you how it was all worth it because now they know how it feels to whiz down a mountain.

Whatever your interests are, you can be sure there are others who share them. There are organizations and societies for everything from radio buffs, beagle breeders, chili cooks, hatpin collectors, and mah-jongg players to puzzle enthusiasts, rhododendron growers, and wine tasters. *The Encyclopedia of Associations*, at your local library, will tell you where to get in touch with just about any interest group you can imagine.

Living on a fixed income should be no deterrent to enjoying your retirement. You can travel off-peak, enjoy matinees and early bird specials, and play golf or tennis on weekdays. There are many discounts available to people over fifty-five. Movies, museums, theaters, sporting events, recreational facilities, adult classes, airlines, hotels, and public transportation often offer discounts. Don't forget to ask before buying a ticket. Carry a photo ID that shows your birthdate. If you don't drive, the motor vehicle bureau in your state will issue you an official identity card.

Learn what resources are available in your community. Look in your local telephone directory under government listings. Senior Centers have the unfortunate reputation of being "day care centers" for the very old and disabled, but a visit to your local Senior Center might surprise you. Most offer a variety of activities, including craft classes, field trips, card tournaments, and foreign-language instruction.

Your local high school may offer adult continuing-education classes. Some communities have adult-education centers and public-recreational facilities that offer all sorts of programs. If you are lucky enough to live near a university, you'll find many interesting classes and activities available to you. Some retirees even relocate near a university just to take advantage of these resources.

Public libraries have become more than book lenders. Many are cultural centers offering lectures, discussions, and movies. You'll also find videotapes, records, compact discs, talking and large-print books, and computer-information systems. Many offer adult literacy programs and home delivery to confined residents.

Museums offer a variety of opportunities for participation. There are exhibits, tours, and special events. Often educational programs, including classes, lectures, discussion groups, field trips, and slide presentations are available. They also provide interesting volunteer options such as fundraising, cataloging, leading tours, or working in the gift shop.

YMCAs, one of America's enduring institutions, continue to provide excellent social and recreational programs to their communities. In the last decade, many have built new facilities and remodeled old to keep up with the demand for their services. Many offer pools, gyms, exercise and weight-lifting equipment, indoor and outdoor tracks, meeting rooms, and classrooms as well as a full range of continuing-education programs, clubs, dances, lectures, concerts, and field trips. In the 1990s, the Y will be making a concerted effort to meet the needs of people over the age of fifty-five. Plans are in the works for special Active Older Adult programs, such as exercise and swimming classes.

Three national senior organizations serve as clearinghouses for information on all sorts of services available to older Americans.

NATIONAL COUNCIL ON AGING

The National Council on Aging, working to improve the quality of life for older people since 1950, can provide you with information on education, arts, humanities, and volunteer opportunities in your community.

National Council on Aging (NCOA)
409 Third Street SW
2nd floor
Washington, DC 20024
(202) 479-1200

NATIONAL COUNCIL OF SENIOR CITIZENS

The National Council of Senior Citizens lobbies for state and federal legislation to benefit older Americans. Among the benefits available to members are travel and tour services and discounts on motels and car rentals.

National Council of Senior Citizens (NCSC)
1331 F Street NW
Washington, DC 20004
(202) 347-8800

American Association of Retired Persons

The American Association of Retired Persons, the largest organization of older people in America, has a membership of more than 32 million. Among its many services is the Institute for Lifelong Learning, a resource center and clearinghouse for continuing education for older people and a volunteer talent bank connecting volunteers to organizations all across the country. Tours, cruises, and discount travel programs, as well as information booklets on many related retirement issues are available to members, as is their bimonthly magazine, *Modern Maturity*.

American Association of Retired Persons (AARP)
601 E Street NW
Washington, DC 20049
(202) 434-2277

CHAPTER II

Volunteering

It's what you do with what you got that pays off
in the end.

WISE OLD OWL*

What bothers people most about retirement is the fear that they will become useless. Yet retirement offers you the greatest opportunity to be of real use. Freed from the need to earn a living, you can focus your energies on what means most to you. What would you like to change in this world? What legacy would you like to leave? After a lifetime of experience, you have a wealth of knowledge and skills to share. There are many ways to put these skills to use. Think of the challenges that face us: homelessness, crime, hunger, disease, destruction of the environment, illiteracy, to mention only some. With so much work needing to be done, how is it possible to have nothing to do?

America has always had a strong tradition of volunteerism, from the barn raisings of colonial times to today's volunteer fire departments. The need for volunteer workers has never been greater than it is now. The 1980s brought drastic cuts in

*Excerpted from "So Dear to My Heart" © The Walt Disney Company. Used by permission.

funding to social-service programs affecting the most vulnerable members of society. Human suffering is no longer isolated to the poorest neighborhoods and special institutions but spills into every community, fills headlines, and confronts us daily. Charitable organizations turn to the public—especially to older Americans—for help.

Older citizens are responding to the call and are serving in many ways. A Harvard law school graduate who never had a chance to use his degree is now a volunteer legal advisor. A widow with an interest in music schedules the practice sessions at her city's concert hall. A retired clothing manufacturer started a clothing program for the homeless (which has reached national proportions) by calling up his cronies and asking for donations. In 1987 alone, 80 million adults gave a total of 19.5 billion volunteer hours valued at about 150 billion dollars. A survey by the American Association of Retired Persons found that 40 percent of older Americans volunteered in 1988; more than half of this group devoted ten or more hours of their time each month. After a decade of apathy and avarice, the 1990s are becoming an age of altruism.

You as a retiree make an excellent volunteer. Your time is your own and can be scheduled around the needs of the cause you serve. You are dependable and loyal, with a highly developed sense of responsibility. You have skills, knowledge, experience, and expertise from which to draw as well as the wisdom and understanding to view your role realistically.

Sharing and caring benefits not only those served but those who serve as well. New evidence supports the many volunteers who claim they experience a "helper's high," similar to the kind of high produced by vigorous exercise. Helpers actually experience identifiable physical sensations characterized by increased body warmth, energy levels, blood flow, and sense of well being. "Helper's high" does not occur when donating money or doing something you feel you must do. The sensation is strongest when the volunteer is in direct contact with the person being helped but recurs, with less intensity, when recalling helping someone. Some researchers believe helping others releases endorphins, the body's natural pain-reducing chemical, which results in good feelings. The sense of calmness that helpers experience is the opposite of stress. Herbert Benson, a famous Harvard cardiologist known for his work on the relaxation response (the body's ability to shift into a deep state of rest) says, "Altruism works...just as yoga, spirituality, and meditation" (*Psychology Today,* October 1988). Some people have been saying it all along: doing good is good for you.

The rawards of volunteering are especially important to retirees. Those things you enjoyed most about work, such as interacting with many different people, working together toward a common goal, meeting challenges, and accomplishing objectives, return with your volunteer career. The loss of identity you felt when you left the work world vanishes and a new sense of purpose and direction can be found. You'll be making new friends and interacting with interesting colleagues. The confusion and depression due to lack of structure and direction that you may have experienced upon retirement will disappear when you schedule regular volunteer hours. With a place to go and people counting on you, it's difficult to feel useless.

Volunteering can have its drawbacks. You must approach your experience with realistic expectations or you may be disappointed. Keep in mind, most volunteer work takes place in a nonprofit world. If you come from a business or corporate background, you may find many things you took for granted in your work environment missing. Adequate facilities, secretarial help, and equipment are often in short supply or altogether absent. If you're used to being the boss, you might find it hard to take direction from the staff in charge. You may not be able to do the kind of work you are used to doing.

Be flexible. Give yourself permission to feel awkward while learning something new. There are a lot more aspects to you than you may think. don't expect to make earthshaking changes or to see people overwhelmed with gratitude. Set realistic goals and enjoy the process of accomplishing them. The rewards of volunteering are not tangible. They aren't counted in dollars and cents. Sometimes you have to look hard to see them. You can no longer measure productivity and accomplishment in terms of salary and job status, but must instead find new ways of looking at success. One volunteer who made a fortune in his business found that the proudest day in his life came when a little child he had helped whispered into his ear, "Thank you."

Approach your volunteer experience as professionally as you would a job. Look around before choosing where you want to work. Interview the staff and observe as much about the facility and program as you can. Remember, you do have rights as a volunteer worker. You have the right to know what is expected of you, what your duties and responsibilities are, to whom and where to report, how much time you are expected to put in, etc. Will you be reimbursed for out-of-pocket expenses? Will lunch and transportation be covered? Will training be provided? Will you be covered by the agency's liability insurance or are there some areas, such as transporting clients in your own car, that might come under your personal insurance? Some volunteer expenses may be tax-deductible. Check with your accountant or local IRS office and remember to keep accurate records.

There are many kinds of volunteer experiences, from ones with highly organized national programs to those of your own invention. The kind of work and types of settings are as varied as the problems in the world. The key to a satisfying volunteer job is finding one that combines your skills and interests. Is there a problem you would like to focus on, or a group of people you wish to work with? Is there something you've always wanted to do but never had the time? What skills do you have that would benefit others? What type of setting would you like to work in? Do you work better in a structured environment or on your own?

Opportunities for volunteering abound in every community. Whether you prefer working directly with people or behind the scenes in administration, many organizations need your services. You don't have to look any further than your local hospital or school to find interesting jobs. Hospital volunteers work as friendly visitors, nurses' aids, and recreation leaders. They bring library carts to patients' bedsides, work in the gift shop, or assist in clerical duties. School volunteers work as teachers' assistants, tutors, playground attendants, and clerical aids.

Religious organizations have highly organized programs to meet the needs of their communities, including assistance to children, the homeless, and the homebound. Social service agencies need help with programs including job development, drug and alcohol abuse counseling, crisis intervention, pre-school care, and assistance for disabled people.

If you are politically minded you might consider working for a political party or candidate. You may wish to become involved in voter registration, special-interest lobbies, or consumer-advocate groups. If saving the environment is your cause, look into recycling programs, activist organizations, or animal rights groups. Parks, zoos, and gardens also welcome volunteers. If culture is your thing, contact your favorite dance company, theater group, museum, orchestra, or library. They always need ushers, or guides, or help in fundraising and public relations.

You need not limit yourself to organized programs. Invent your own job. Every day on his way to work in New York City's garment district and again on his way home at night, Richard Lewin was disturbed by the sight of children from the welfare hotels running unsupervised through the streets. When he retired, he decided to do something for these children. He approached the parks department with the idea of running special events for them. His first event was a harvest festival. He convinced local merchants to donate apples, pumpkins, and doughnuts. He arranged for a hay wagon and a country blue grass band—complete with square dance callers—to make appearances. Children from all over the city enjoyed a day in the country in the middle of Central Park. Now Mr. Lewin has his own office at the parks department and runs special events for the city on a regular basis.

No matter what your interests, skills, or abilities, there is a job for you. The following listing will give you some examples of the many opportunities available.

VOLUNTEER CLEARINGHOUSES

Almost every town has a government agency that acts as a clearinghouse for local volunteer opportunities. Check with your mayor's office or your town's chamber of commerce for your local voluntary action center or bureau. Listings in local telephone directories may be categorized under a variety of names beginning with the words volunteer or voluntary. Religious organizations and civic associations are other good sources for referrals.

THE NATIONAL VOLUNTEER CENTER

The National VOLUNTEER Center works to enhance the abilities of people to address community problems through volunteering and supports the effectiveness of local volunteer centers which serve as clearinghouses. They can refer you to your local volunteer center and provide information booklets on volunteering.

The National VOLUNTEER Center
Suite 500
1111 North 19th Street
Arlington, VA 22209
(703) 276-0542

UNITED WAY

The United Way has hundreds of national and community-based centers that match applicants with volunteer options. Look in your telephone directory for the United Way nearest you.

AMERICAN ASSOCIATION OF RETIRED PERSONS (AARP)

The motto of the American Association of Retired Persons is "To serve, not to be served." This philosophy is demonstrated by the almost four hundred thousand volunteers who work in a variety of AARP programs around the country, helping others deal with crucial issues. AARP volunteers provide information and counseling on housing options, retirement planning, widowhood, tax preparation, and health, legal, and financial issues. They also work toward reversing age discrimination.

The American Association of Retired Persons operates a Volunteer Talent Bank that connects volunteers to organizations. After completing a registration form that identifies interests and skills, volunteer applicants are told about suitable volunteer positions in their community.

For further information write to AARP for their Volunteer Talent Bank brochure (D12329):

Volunteer Talent Bank
American Association of Retired Persons
601 E Street NW
Washington, DC 20049

ACTION

Action, the primary federal domestic volunteer organization, was created in 1971 out of President John F. Kennedy's Peace

Corps concept to promote the spirit and practice of volunteering. Today more than a half million volunteers serve in local Action programs around the country, providing vital services to their communities. The majority of these volunteers are older Americans who use the talents and skills developed over a lifetime to confront such problems as illiteracy, homelessness, drug abuse, abused and abandoned children, and the needs of the homebound elderly. Action and the many programs it administers prove again and again that the strength of America lies in our rich heritage of neighbor helping neighbor and that the solution to our problems begins by cleaning up our own backyards.

For information on Action programs, contact your regional recruiting office.

Region I
Room 473
10 Causeway Street
Boston, MA
02222-1039
(617) 565-7000

Region II
Room 758
6 World Trade
Center
New York, NY
10048-0206
(212) 466-3481

Region III
Room 108
US Customs House
2nd and Chestnut
Streets
Philadelphia, PA
19106-2912
(215) 597-9972

Region IV
Room 1003
101 Marietta
Street, NW
Atlanta, GA
30323-2301
(404) 331-2859

Region V
6th Floor
10 West Jackson
Boulevard
Chicago, IL
60604-3964
(312) 353-5107

Region VI
Room 6B11
1100 Commerce
Street
Dallas, TX
75242-0696
(214) 767-9494

Region VIII	*Region IX*	*Region X*
Suite 2930	Room 530	Suite 3039
Executive Tower	211 Main Street	Federal Office
Building	San Francisco, CA	Building
1405 Curtis Street	94105-1914	909 First Avenue
Denver, CO	(415) 974-0673	Seattle, WA
80202-2349		98174-1103
(303) 844-2671		(206) 442-1558

RETIRED SENIOR VOLUNTEER PROGRAM (RSVP)

RSVP is the largest of the Action programs. It offers a wide range of opportunities for people over sixty to use their talents and experience in service to their communities. Operating through grants to public and nonprofit organizations, it refers volunteers to hundreds of community service programs throughout the country. Assignments are varied and range from crime prevention and tutoring refugees to manning "hotlines" and assisting probation officers. Whatever the assignment, RSVP volunteers make important contributions to the welfare of their communities and are rewarded with a strong sense of their own personal worth. Transportation and on-duty accident and liability insurance is provided. Volunteers are reimbursed for meals and expenses.

VOLUNTEERS IN SERVICE TO AMERICA (VISTA)

VISTA requires a full-time year-long commitment; its projects aim to assist low-income people improve the quality of their lives. VISTA volunteers live and work among the poor, serving in urban areas, rural areas, and on Indian reservations in the United States, Puerto Rico, Guam, and the Virgin Islands. VISTA provides drug abuse counseling, literacy tutoring, employment training, food distribution, shelter for the homeless, and neighborhood revitalization assistance. Its volunteers must be US citizens in good health with the specific skills and abilities required by the community organization requesting help. Training is provided. A monthly allowance to cover housing, food, medical care, and travel expenses is paid. Upon completion of duty, volunteers receive a stipend for each month of service.

SENIOR COMPANION PROGRAM (SCP)

Based on the philosophy that the best way to help people is to help them help each other, the Senior Companion Program offers opportunities for low-income persons age sixty or over to provide care and companionship to the homebound elderly. By doing what friends do for friends—visiting, sharing a meal, talking about old times, providing helpful suggestions—Senior Companions help their peers maintain their independence. Forty hours of training prepare Senior Companions to be the vital link between those they visit and the community services and resources that can make a positive difference in their lives. To make it possible to devote four hours a day, five days a week, to their work, volunteers receive an annual stipend that is nontaxable and does not affect social security or disability payments. Volunteers are also reimbursed for transportation and meals and are provided with on-duty insurance and an annual physical exam. Though these benefits are important to low-income volunteers, the real rewards are being needed and appreciated.

FOSTER GRANDPARENTS PROGRAM (FGP)

Across the country, hundreds of thousands of severely retarded, emotionally disturbed, physically handicapped, troubled, or abandoned children are shuttled into institutions barely able to provide basic care. Due to limited resources, such institutions cannot provide the personal attention, support, and encouragement these children need. Foster Grandparents can. Their job is to give the love and attention that is lacking in these institutional environments. Five days a week, four hours a day, Foster Grandparents provide companionship and guidance to two assigned "grandchildren." The bond that develops between the children and the volunteers nurtures both. The volunteers find new purpose and meaning in their lives and the children find hope in the knowledge that someone cares.

Low-income persons age sixty and over are eligible to serve. After forty hours of pre-service training, volunteers are assigned to supervised child-care teams within the agencies. Volunteers receive a modest tax-free stipend and transportation allowance to cover volunteering costs as well as hot meals while on the job, accident liability insurance, and an annual physical examination.

PEACE CORPS

The Peace Corps, once synonymous with youth, is aging. When President Kennedy founded the Peace Corps in 1961, he sounded a trumpet that called thousands of idealistic youth to serve two-year terms in underdeveloped countries. But the baby-boomers have babies of their own now, and today's college population is more concerned with the practicalities of making a living than in sharing the vision of the 1960s activists. So the Peace Corps, looking for new volunteers, is actively recruiting older Americans. They are especially interested in people with skills in science, education, agriculture, engineering, the trades, forestry, fisheries, and community development. Today's retirees make excellent candidates. They are free from financial and family responsibilities, have a wealth of skills and experience to share as well as perspective on what can be accomplished. Participating countries have a high regard and respect for age and welcome the assistance of elders. But the Peace Corps is not for everyone. Only the hardy and adventurous need apply. It means being very far from home and family, in rugged living conditions, in such places as Africa, Asia, the Caribbean, Central America, and the Pacific for two years. It also means the once-in-a-lifetime experience of viewing the world from a whole new perspective and of putting into someone else's hands the tools that will improve their lives.

Write or call the Peace Corps for more information. A free booklet entitled "Senior Volunteers in the Peace Corps" answers the most commonly asked questions by Peace Corps applicants fifty years and over.

Peace Corps
Public Response Unit
1990 K Street NW
Washington, DC 20562
(800) 602-3000

SERVICE CORPS OF RETIRED EXECUTIVES (SCORE)

When Joseph Friedman closed his manufacturing business after forty years, he felt he'd had enough pressure for a lifetime and decided to devote all of his time to his favorite sport, golf. But when he wasn't golfing he felt restless and began looking for ways to volunteer his time. At first, he tried working with school children, but found that working one-on-one with a child wasn't for him. Then someone told him about the Service Corps of Retired Executives, which uses the expertise and experience of retired professionals to assist fledgling businesses solve their problems. For the past nine years, for three days a week, he has been putting his business skills to work advising people with business problems or those who wish to begin their own businesses. The other four days he golfs.

SCORE was founded in 1964 under the auspices of the Small Business Administration to provide free management assistance to small-business owners. In addition to one-on-one counseling, many SCORE chapters conduct seminars and workshops on business planning. SCORE offers an excellent opportunity for successful businesspeople to put their managerial, professional, or technical expertise to work.

For further information, contact your local chapter of the Small Business Administration.

LEAGUE OF WOMEN VOTERS

The League of Women Voters has roots in the women's suffrage movement and traces its conception to 1840 when Lucretia Mott and Elizabeth Cady Stanton were denied seats at the World Anti-Slavery Convention in London because they were women. But it is not for women only: men are welcome to join this nonpartisan organization whose primary purpose is to promote informed and active citizen participation in government. Its work includes public education and information, voter registration, and lobbying for political change on issues for which there is membership agreement.

The League of Women Voters offers exciting avenues of public involvement for politically minded retirees. Most of the work of the League is accomplished through voluntary effort. Volunteers chair committees; prepare publications; run voter-registration, membership, and fundraising drives; and maintain a year-round telephone information service educating the public about issues related to government and voting. The League keeps its members actively involved in politics by studying issues, holding discussions, and agreeing on positions for action.

Pauline Hechtman (seventy-nine years old) has been a member for twenty years. Before retiring, she was principal, for sixteen years, of an elementary school in Brooklyn's Brownsville section. She is vice president of the New York League, a voluntary but full-time occupation. Her work at the League calls on her administrative and educational skills; meanwhile, she is constantly learning more about American politics. Recently, she addressed a group of Chinese college students interested in American political processes. Constant exchange of information and ideas makes Pauline's job at the League exciting and challenging.

If you would like to join, call the League office listed in your local telephone directory or contact their national headquarters.

League of Women Voters in the US
1730 M Street NW
Washington, DC 20036
(202) 429-1965

AMERICAN RED CROSS

For over one hundred years, the American Red Cross has been there when we needed them. When disaster strikes—be it fire, flood, hurricane, or tornado—the Red Cross provides food, clothing, shelter, and other emergency services to disaster victims. This agency reaches into every community in the world, wherever victims of war or natural disaster need help.

Much of the Red Cross's work takes place behind the scenes, preventing disasters before they happen. Red Cross health and safety workers assist with life-saving programs, such as blood-pressure testing, AIDS education, first-aid stations at public events, water safety monitoring, home health aid, parenting education, and classes in CPR. Nearly half of America's blood supply is collected by the Red Cross. Other programs concentrate on the needs of the military, the young, the elderly, and the homeless.

If you would like to join the American Red Cross, contact

the chapter listed in your local telephone directory or write to their national headquarters.

American Red Cross
National Headquarters
Washington, DC 20006

VOLUNTEERS IN TECHNICAL ASSISTANCE (VITA)

People with technical skills to share can become VITA volunteers. VITA was established by a group of scientists and engineers to provide developing countries with technical assistance. VITA receives thousands of requests daily for information on agriculture, small-enterprise development, low-cost housing, reforestation, water-supply management, and sanitation. These requests are matched with an appropriately skilled volunteer from within VITA's computerized file. Most inquiries can be answered by mail, with consultants providing evaluations, designs, analyses, or guidelines. Though occasionally VITA volunteers work on-site, they more frequently serve on technical panels, write and review publications, and formulate promotional strategies.

To become a VITA volunteer, call or write:

Volunteers in Technical Assistance
Suite 200
1815 North Lynn Street
Arlington, VA 22209
(703) 276-1800

INTERNATIONAL EXECUTIVE SERVICE CORPS (IESC)

When demand for the Philippine Phosphate Fertilizer company's products outgrew shipping facilities, they turned to the

International Executive Service Corps for help. IESC recruited Allen Cameron of Essex, Connecticut, a retired executive vice president of National Bulk Carriers. Allen had more than fifty years of experience in marine transportation. His recommendations included redesigning a pier and establishing a procedure for off-site bagging. He put the company back on track and made it possible for them to export seven hundred fifty tons of fertilizer to 11 countries.

For more than twenty-five years, the IESC has recruited retired, highly skilled business executives and technical advisors to help developing countries. Oversees clients requesting specific advice are matched with American business executives whose expertise suits the project. Voluntary advisors work on short-term assignments, providing guidance and assistance around the world.

More than seven hundred executives are selected yearly to share their expertise with developing countries. Most projects last from two to three months. Volunteers may travel with their spouses and receive travel expenses and a per diem.

International Executive Service Corps
8 Stamford Forum, PO Box 10005
Stamford, CT 06904-2005
(203) 967-6000

INTERGENERATIONAL PROGRAMS

The extended family, with its mix of generations, once provided a natural support system that sustained the varying economic, educational, and emotional needs of its members. But rapid social changes, including the mobility of the nuclear family, divorce, single-parent homes, and two-career couples have reshaped the American family. Isolation of generations is now the norm. Children are segregated in schools, adults at work, and older adults in housing. As a result, society suffers from misunderstandings and conflicts between generations that have lost a sense of mutual support. Intergenerational programs combat these problems by bringing younger and older people together for mutually beneficial exchanges.

Today more than ever, our younger generation needs the guidance and support of those who are older and wiser. Studies show that 10 to 15 percent of young Americans between the ages of sixteen and nineteen are considered at risk of becoming "disconnected" from society due to pregnancy, dropping out of school, illiteracy, poverty, and alcohol and drug abuse. The future for many of these children is bleak, ending too often in early death from suicide, homicide, automobile accidents, or drug overdoses. Yet it is possible to change these statistics. If these children can be motivated to value themselves and believe in their own potential, their chances of becoming productive members of society will increase.

TEAM WORK

Team Work, a project of the Foundation for Exceptional Children, uses the expertise and experience of older Americans to address the needs of young people at risk. Young people ages eighteen to twenty-five with learning disabilities, physical impairments, sensory limitations, or mild retardation are teamed up with volunteers who serve as mentors or job coaches. Each volunteer works one-on-one with a young person to help identify his or her marketable skills and interests and assists in locating employment opportunities.

Team Work
Foundation for Exceptional Children
1920 Association Drive
Reston, VA 22091
(703) 620-1054

FAMILY FRIENDS PROJECT

The Family Friends Project trains volunteers fifty-five and over to help families with children who have chronic illnesses or disabilities cope with the pressures of caring for such children. The volunteers spend a minimum of four hours a week as a companion for the child and a helper to the parent. Family Friend volunteers become an important person to all members of the family, not just to the disabled child. The presence of another adult in the home gives the parents a welcome break from the constant demands of caring for such children and gives the other siblings a chance to get special attention. Family Friends frequently become surrogate parents to the children's parents as well as surrogate grandparents to the children.

Family Friends Project
National Council on Aging
409 Third Street SW
Washington, DC 20024
(202) 479-6675

SCHOOL VOLUNTEERS

Schools everywhere need the assistance of dedicated volunteers to help meet special challenges. Schools are under tremendous pressure to prepare students for a world requiring technical skills, but at the same time they must make do with low budgets, overcrowded facilities, and overworked teachers. Children today, meanwhile, must cope with crime, drug addiction, divorce, disease, and poverty.

Schools need the help of experienced adults who can give children the attention and guidance overworked teachers cannot. The presence of older volunteers in the classroom can give young children comfort, stability, and a feeling of emotional safety. Older children benefit from the presence of mentors and role models during the confusing years of adolescence. Volunteers find the enthusiasm and openness of children stimulating and enjoy sharing their life experiences with the younger generation while knowing their influence could mean the difference between a wasted life and a successful one.

If you wish to serve a few hours a week or several hours a day, your local school can use your help. If you would like to work directly with children, you can help in after-school programs, befriend a lonely child, chaperone field trips, or tutor a child needing extra help. Behind the scenes, you can catalogue and repair books in the library, serve on special committees, coordinate fundraising events, or set up science projects. There are even opportunities for homebound individuals to contribute by helping with holiday decorations and bulletin board displays, or by making friendly telephone calls to "latchkey" children.

For information about volunteer programs in your community, contact your school superintendent's office or write to AARP for their booklet, "Becoming a School Partner" (Publication D13527).

American Association of Retired Persons
Program Department
Special Projects Section
601 E Street NW
Washington, DC 20049

Court Appointed Special Advocates (CASA)

Every child deserves a stable home. But for many foster-care children, home is a succession of changing environments. Living with the constant threat of change causes anguish for children already suffering trauma. Most are in foster care because their parents neglected, abused, or abandoned them, or because their parents were unable to care for them. Without family stability, these children may have futures clouded by delinquency and crime, and they may become child abusers themselves.

Recognizing this problem, federal and state laws mandate judicial reviews of foster-care cases. But courts are overwhelmed. Sometimes judges hear seventy cases a day; they don't always get enough information to make the best possible recommendations. The job of Court Appointed Special Advocates is to investigate all aspects of a child's living situation and make recommendations to the court.

CASA serves a very important function. They deal with only one or two children at a time, and are able to construct a better picture of the child's situation than overloaded caseworkers can. During an investigation, CASA volunteers speak with the parents, foster parents, social workers, neighbors, doctors, teachers, and the child himself, gathering better information for the judge so that the court decision will serve the best interests of the child.

As a child passes from one caretaker to the next, their deepest needs can go unattended. But an astute CASA worker is often able to pick up what others overlook. Haywood L. Green has been a CASA worker since his retirement from the postal service five years ago. Mr. Green understands the needs of young people His own troubled youth caused him to leave the South when he was only sixteen; eventually, he settled in Harlem. He considers himself a lucky man, having survived both World War II and the Korean War, and wants to give something back. One of his cases involved a five-year-old girl who lived with her grandmother in an apartment without electricity. One day, the candles they used started a fire that left the girl's arm badly scarred. The child was deeply self-conscious about the scar, but none of the social service agencies involved with her case did anything about it. Except Haywood. He knew of a burn clinic run by the Shriners for patients unable to pay. After nine months of red tape, he obtained treatment for the child. Now, almost a teenager, she no longer hides under long-sleeved shirts and is a much happier and more outgoing child. Haywood says working with CASA is the most rewarding experience he has ever had.

Court Appointed Special Advocates are citizen volunteers trained and supervised by professional staff. Previous experience in such fields as child development, drug abuse counseling, and work with the retarded is helpful but not essential. Objective and independent thinking, good communication skills, impartiality, sensitivity to families under stress, dedication to doing a thorough job, and the ability to remain active during a case's entire litigation period are required.

There are more than four hundred CASA programs in forty-seven states working to ensure that every child has the best home situation possible. Programs may go under different names, such as Pro-Kids, Child Advocates, Guardian Ad Litem programs, or Child Advocate Services. For information on the CASA program nearest you, contact their national headquarters.

National CASA Association
2722 Eastlake Avenue East
Seattle, WA 98102
(206) 328-8588

SAVE THE EARTH

Saving our planet from environmental destruction may be the ultimate challenge of the decade. Some scientists believe that given our present direction, our planet will become unlivable in less than one hundred years. Others say that through innovation and concerted effort we can eliminate the main sources of our problems in one generation.

Faced with the overwhelming problems of acid rain, global

warming, deforestation, the destruction of the ozone layer, and the garbage glut, it is easy to feel hopeless and assume the inevitability of doom. But we are not helpless. People can make a difference. The tenacity and determination of one retiree saved Protection Island, a refuge for three-quarters of the seabirds in Puget Sound, from the hands of developers. Eleanor Stopps' crusade took almost ten years, lots of hard work, and much disappointment, but ended in the passing of a congressional bill insuring the protection of the island. People have brought about other changes. The Earth Island Institute and individual consumers encouraged the nation's three largest canners of tuna to stop buying fish caught in nets that also trap and kill dolphins. The bald eagle, once endangered by DDT, has increased in population nearly sevenfold in recent years. Fish have returned to Lake Erie. Yet there is no doubt that the earth is still in serious trouble and needs much help.

Opportunities for action are abundant. Your community may have a recycling program that needs your help. Or you could start one. What aspect of the environment interests you most? Do you have a favorite lake in which you like to fish? Is it still pollution-free? Are animals your main concern? Contact your local ASPCA or animal rights group. Perhaps you like to garden? Start a local tree-planting program or help in the public gardens. When you begin to explore the many ways you can help make the world healthier for future generations, you will no longer feel part of the problem but will become part of the solution.

Some of the organizations active in environmental issues that can use your help are described below.

GREENPEACE

The Goal of the Worldwide Greenpeace Movement is preserving the earth and all the life it supports. To accomplish this, Greenpeace works to end the threat of nuclear war and the production of nuclear weapons, to protect the environment from nuclear and toxic pollution, to stop the threat of global warming, and to end the needless slaughter of endangered animals. The Greenpeace Movement believes in nonviolent confrontation while taking direct action to stop environmental abuse. Greenpeace primarily works through grassroots lobbying but also uses nonconventional tactics, such as plugging discharge pipes of chemical polluters or using highspeed, inflatable crafts to interfere with whalers and sealers.

Greenpeace Action, which handles grassroots lobbying and related activities in support of Greenpeace's US work, has made significant contributions. Working with citizen groups, it defeated proposed municipal solid-waste incinerators and instituted comprehensive recycling programs in cities including Seattle, Los Angeles, and Boston. In 1989, Greenpeace Action collected 250,000 signatures supporting a comprehensive test-ban treaty. It helped close the Savannah River Plant reactors in South Carolina and the Hanford Reservation N-reactor and PUREX reprocessing facility in Washington.

Greenpeace welcomes volunteers and hopes to provide as meaningful an experience as possible. Volunteers are needed to assist with member correspondence, daily maintenance of press files, data entry, and preparation and distribution of campaign and educational materials. There are also volunteer internships available in the areas of ocean ecology, disarmament, toxics issues, media and magazines, and legal issues.

For information contact the Greenpeace Action Regional Office nearest you.

Chicago:
1017 West Jackson Boulevard
Chicago, IL 60607
(312) 666-3305

Boston:
709 Center Street
Jamaica Plain
Boston, MA 02130
(617) 983-0300

Seattle:
4649 Sunnyside Avenue North
Seattle, WA 98103
(206) 632-4326

Florida:
Wilton Plaza, Suite 80
1881 NE 26th Street
Wilton Manors, FL 32240
(305) 561-2705

San Francisco:
Port Mason, Building E
San Francisco, CA 94123
(415) 474-6767

National Headquarters:
Greenpeace USA
1436 U Street NW
Washington, DC 20009
(202) 462-1177

GLOBAL RELEAF

Many scientists believe that the earth's temperature is rising. The 1980s were the warmest years on record. If the earth's temperatures continue to rise, the consequences could be cataclysmic. If the polar ice cap melts and oceans rise, coastal cities could become submerged, effectively vanishing. Heat and drought could turn farms into deserts.

The burning of fuel to meet mankind's energy needs releases carbon dioxide, which traps the sun's energy in the atmosphere; gradually, the earth will turn into a greenhouse. The industrialized countries are the main producers of greenhouse gases (the United States is the largest producer, followed by the Soviet Union). But the developing countries already account for 45 percent of such emissions and their contribution will most likely rise as their need for energy increases. To compound the problem, tropical forests, which play an important role in replacing oxygen and regulating global climate, are disappearing at a rate of one acre every half second as trees are cut for timber and to clear land for development.

Global Releaf attempts to combat the greenhouse effect by planting trees. Trees turn carbon dioxide into oxygen. They also reduce our need for energy by cooling our homes with their shade and offering relief in urban environments where expanses of pavement create "heat islands." They filter out air pollution, reduce noise pollution, prevent soil erosion, provide a habitat for wildlife, and improve the aesthetics of our surroundings.

Give the earth a helping hand: plant a tree. Trees planted properly around your home will reduce your heat and air-conditioning bills by providing shade and windbreak. Get your community involved. Plant or replace trees in public areas. You'll improve the appearance of your neighborhood while doing something to save the earth.

The American Forestry Association is prepared to help you. They'll send you information on planting trees or organizing a tree-planting project in your community.

Global Releaf
American Forestry Association
PO Box 2000
Washington, DC 20013
(202) 667-3300

Sierra Club

For nearly a century, the Sierra Club has been an important champion of environmental causes. Through a strong activist network, it works as a political force pressuring for solutions to the environmental problems facing us. If you would like to take on this challenge, the Sierra Club can provide you with resources to work toward solving the environmental issues that most interest you. They can supply background information, posters, audiovisual materials, practical guides, and team you up with others interested in your causes.

The Sierra Club Sourcebook is a comprehensive catalogue of educational materials including books, posters, and guides. You can learn such things as how to become an environmental activist, how to influence public policy, what you can do at home to protect the environment, and how your everyday purchases can help make a better world.

Sierra Club Sourcebook
Public Affairs
730 Polk Street
San Francisco, CA 94109
(415) 776-2211

National Audubon Society

If you are interested in working toward protecting the environment, the National Audubon Society provides an organized, effective way to focus your energies. They can supply the tools, information, and support you need to get started and put you in touch with a network of people with similar values.

The National Audubon Society has been a strong force for wildlife conservation for more than seventy-five years. Its voice is well respected by government and industry. It is one of the largest national environmental membership organizations. Its members are part of an international group of conservationists working within local communities to help save endangered species, protect natural areas and wildlife habitats, and develop environmental educational programs.

When you join the National Audubon Society, you automatically become a member of your local chapter. As a member you may participate in natural-history field trips, attend films and lectures, and work on current issues along with other people. You may attend Audubon's Summer Ecology Camps and Workshops and be admitted free of charge to most National Audubon Nature Centers. You receive your chapter's newsletter and *Audubon* magazine. You can also join the activist network and receive the bi-monthly newsletter, *Audubon Activist*, keeping you informed about critical environmental issues. Your membership contribution helps support Audubon's work in scientific research, environmental wildlife education, and the maintenance of wildlife sanctuaries.

National Audubon Society
950 Third Avenue
New York, NY 10022
(212) 546-9305

VOLUNTEERS IN PARKS (VIPS)

Since 1872, when Yellowstone became our first national park, Americans have been privileged to enjoy the beauty of their natural heritage in the environments protected by our National Park System. Today, more than three hundred fifty national parks provide oases from civilization's crush. With industrialization threatening to choke our ecosystems, these natural treasures have never been more important. Just as our generation needs a refuge from the stresses of modern life, so too will future generations.

VIPS play an important part in preserving and protecting our national parks. There are many different jobs available, such as maintaining trails, counting wildlife, guiding tours, answering mail, maintaining park libraries, and driving shuttle buses. The length of assignments ranges from a few hours a week to a full-time commitment for an entire season or even year-round. Volunteer opportunities are outlined in a free booklet, "Volunteers in Parks," available from the National Parks Service. You may request one at a park near you.

VOLUNTEER VACATIONS

Volunteer vacations are short-term voluntary commitments combining the adventure of traveling with the joy of sharing. You might construct new bridges in New Hampshire's White Mountains or study ancient costumes in Greece. Volunteer vacations provide the opportunity to work with people from all over the world on exciting projects while building strong friendships and lasting memories. Most programs last two to three weeks and require no skills other than flexibility, stamina, and willingness to live in a communal environment. Except for digs and scientific expeditions, where you share in the cost of the study, most volunteer vacations only require you to pay transportation and registration fees. Living expenses are covered by the sponsoring organizations; most expenses are tax-deductible.

University Research Expedition Program (UREP)

Delbert Raby, a retired Boy Scout executive from California, has gone on seven University Research Expeditions and plans to go on more. He has looked for 40-million-year-old insects embedded in amber in the Dominican Republic, studied the funeral customs of the Tongas on an island near Fiji, dug for artifacts of hunter-gatherers in southern Chile, and studied Mayan dwellings in Belize. He loves the joy of discovery and the satisfaction of contributing to worthwhile projects, but the best part, he says, is the people he meets and the friendships he makes.

Share in the challenges and rewards of scientific discovery. Join one of more than twenty University of California research teams that head out each summer for a two- to three-week adventure in exotic international destinations. Under the guidance of these researchers, volunteer participants investigate everything from endangered pelicans in California to traditional textiles of Bolivia. You might examine plant life in the vanishing Equadorian rain forest, explore the problems of AIDS and homeless youth in Rio de Janeiro, or study the changing strains of traditional Turkish music among guest workers in Berlin. With the objective of improving people's lives and preserving the world's resources, projects span a variety of disciplines, including archaeology, botany, sociology, animal behavior, and marine studies. A catalogue of upcoming expeditions is available.

Participants in UREP expeditions contribute to their expenses, which makes the research possible. The amount qualifies as a charitable tax deduction. Most projects do not require previous experience.

University Research Expeditions Program
Desk L-02
University of California
Berkeley, CA 94720
(415) 642-6586

FOUNDATION FOR FIELD RESEARCH

Have you ever dreamed of being an archaeologist, oceanographer, or naturalist? As a contributing member of the Foundation for Field Research, you can realize these dreams. You might study tool use among chimpanzees in Africa, unearth ancient dwellings in Italy, investigate prehistoric garbage in New York, or dive for data on the mating practices of the ocellated wrasse off the coast of France.

You do not need previous experience, only a time commitment of two days to one month, stamina for hard work, and the ability to make a tax-deductible contribution to pay your expenses and help cover the cost of the expedition. You will receive a preparatory booklet describing the research subject and methods. Once in the field, you will be given instruction from a researcher. A field manager will accompany the trip and assist with logistics.

Foundation for Field Research
PO Box 2010
Alpine, CA 92001
(619) 445-9264

EARTHWATCH

Earthwatch recruits volunteers to contribute physical and financial assistance to scientists on research expeditions around the world. Its trips have been called "short-term scientific Peace Corps" because they provide opportunities to help solve some of the critical environmental questions facing us today.

Earthcorps volunteers have made significant contributions. With the help of Earthcorps volunteers hauling gunnysacks of swamp soil, Dr. Terry Erwin of the Smithsonian Institution demonstrated that, instead of slashing and burning rain forests to clear land for farming, an ancient Mayan technique of intensive gardening could produce vegetables in stationary raised beds. Endangered species such as the leatherback turtle have been helped in their struggle to survive through the assistance of Earthcorps volunteers, who weighed them, tagged their flippers, mapped where they buried their eggs, and, if they were too close to the water, reburied them in safer spots.

Each year, hundreds of projects need assistance in the areas of rain forest conservation, ecology, arts and archaeology, geosciences, life sciences, marine studies, and social sciences. Volunteers share the cost of research expeditions, which averaged $1,300 in 1990. All expedition costs are in support of scientific research and are tax-deductible. The dividends to Earthwatch investors include the pride of contributing to scientific advancement and the personal satisfaction of discovery, adventure, and friendship.

Earthwatch
PO Box 403N
680 Mount Auburn Street
Watertown, MA 02272
(617) 926-8200

AMERICAN HIKING SOCIETY VOLUNTEER VACATIONS

Wake at dawn to the splendor of a mountain sunrise, breakfast beside an open fire, hike deep into the woods, and spend the day cutting and clearing a new trail. Then relax in the evening with conversation around a campfire. If you are an experienced backpacker capable of hiking five to ten miles a day and are comfortable living in primitive conditions, then the American Hiking Society's Volunteer Vacations are for you.

Each year, the American Hiking Society sends teams of volunteers deep into parks to help protect and preserve America's forests. Each team has six to fifteen volunteers ranging in age from thirteen to seventy. Most projects last ten days and are in remote areas to which the team must hike and make camp. Work areas might be on an island in the Pacific or the Green Mountain National Forest in Vermont. You could blaze a six-mile trail in the Routt National Forest in Yampa, Colorado, climb a volcano in Maui in search of endangered plants, or paint cabins in the wilderness of Hasselborg Lake, Alaska.

Most of the work is done in summer, but a few projects go on during spring and fall also. You must supply your own equipment and pay for transportation. These expenses are tax-deductible. Upon acceptance, you will be charged a $30 registration fee. For free information about the programs, send a stamped, self-addressed, business-sized envelope to AHS.

AHS Volunteer Vacations
PO Box 86
North Scituate, MA 02060

HEIFER PROJECT INTERNATIONAL

Half the world goes to bed hungry. Each day, thirty-five thousand people die of starvation. Most are children. Twenty-four people will die of hunger while you read this page. Heifer Project International's mission is to relieve hunger, not with a cup but a cow. Through the gift of livestock, they provide food, income, and self-reliance for the starving people of the world.

HPI solves the problem of hunger one family at a time. Organized groups of farmers in needy countries and in the United States are supplied with food-producing animals, including dairy and beef cattle, goats, sheep, pigs, rabbits, fish, honeybees, poultry, buffalo, camels, and yaks and are taught to care for and manage these animals. Each person who is helped must pass on the gift, providing a needy neighbor with an off-spring of his animal, thereby establishing a life-sustaining chain.

HPI welcomes your involvement. You can go to their learning and livestock center in Perryville, Arkansas, and spend a day learning about fighting hunger. You can spend a week at their ranch, tending the animals, repairing the facilities, cooking meals, or conducting tours. The 1,225-acre ranch in the rolling hills of Arkansas offers comfortable housing and rewarding work as well as the simple pleasures of a country lifestyle.

Heifer Project International
International Learning and Livestock Center
Route 2, Box 33
Perryville, AR 72126
(501) 889-5124

Heifer Project International Headquarters
PO Box 808
Little Rock, AR 72201
(501) 376-6836

SERVICE CIVIL INTERNATIONAL VOLUNTARY SERVICE

SCI promotes world peace, bringing volunteers from around the world to work on a wide variety of projects in the United States and Europe. They work in work camps which take place mostly between July and September and last between two to four weeks. Teams are of varying ages and from all over the world. As an SCI volunteer you might restore a farmhouse in central Illinois, assist the handicapped at Camp Courageous in Iowa, or work to correct pollution damage in the Himalayas.

SCI provides room and board during camp. Volunteers pay for transportation and out-of-pocket expenses.

To apply, send $3.00 for overseas work camp descriptions or a business-sized, self-addressed stamped envelope for US camp information to:

SCI-USA
Rt. 2, Box 506
Innis Free Village
Crozet, VA 22932
(804) 823-1826

PUBLICATIONS

AARP RESOURCES FOR VOLUNTEERING

The American Association of Retired Persons publishes free information booklets on volunteering. For single copies, send a postcard, making sure to note the publication's name and stock number to:

AARP Fulfillment Center
601 E Street NW
Washington, DC 20049

"Community Service Project Packet." Publication D13669.
A practical guide to opportunities for volunteer involvement, including health, consumer action, community safety, environmental, and intergenerational activities.

"To Serve Not to Be Served." Publication D12028.
A guide to volunteer work with insights on what it means to be a volunteer.

"Volunteer Opportunities for Your Congregation." Publication D12612.
Information on volunteer programs of interest to congregations, including Widowed Persons Service, the Citizen Representation Program, Reminiscence, and Tax-Aid Program.

"Making America Literate: How You Can Help." Publication D12755.
Get involved in the national fight against illiteracy. This booklet includes a list of organizations working to combat this problem.

VOLUNTEER, A CIEE ANNUAL GUIDE

The Council on Educational Exchange publishes a comprehensive annual guide to voluntary service in the US and abroad entitled *Volunteer! The Comprehensive Guide to Voluntary Service in the U.S. and Abroad*. It lists hundreds of volunteer opportunities as far away as Africa or as close as your hometown. Whatever your interests or skills, there is an abundance of ways you can reach out to others. You can help heal the sick, feed the hungry, befriend the lonely, or care for the earth. Spend a weekend, a month, or a year engaged in rewarding, productive activity that will enrich your life and the lives of others.

For a copy of *Volunteer* send CIEE a certified check or money order for $6.95, plus $1.00 postage for book-rate mailing, $2.50 for first class. (New York residents must include sales tax.)

Council on International Educational Exchange (CIEE)
Department ISS-18
205 East 42nd Street
New York, NY 10017
(212) 661-1414

HELPING OUT IN THE OUTDOORS

Perhaps you would enjoy improving America's parks, forests, or other public lands. *Helping Out in the Outdoors,* the American Hiking Society's directory of volunteer work and internships, lists hundreds of rewarding opportunities around the country for outdoor enthusiasts seeking to share their love for nature. You may, for example, spend time as a fire lookout at Kootenai National Forest in Montana, a canoe instructor at Pamlico River in North Carolina, or a campground host at Great Sand Dunes National Monument in Colorado.

Send the American Hiking Society a check or money order for $5.00 for a single copy of *Helping Out in the Outdoors,* or $15.00 for a three-year subscription.

American Hiking Society (AHS)
1015 31st Street NW
Washington, DC 20007
(703) 385-3252

Directory of National Citizen Volunteer Environmental-Monitoring Programs

Published by the Environmental Protection Agency (EPA), this directory contains a listing of monitoring programs around the country. Special emphasis is placed on water-quality monitoring programs, such as Idaho's Citizens Volunteer Monitoring Program, where volunteers are trained to collect water-quality samples from Idaho's lakes and rivers. National programs include the National Audubon Society's Christmas Bird Count, where more than forty-two thousand volunteers inventory bird populations around the world, and the Cooperative Weather Observer Program, sponsored by the National Weather Service, which employs more than eleven thousand volunteers to record rainfall, snowfall, and temperatures throughout the United States. Each listing includes a brief description of the program and notation of the contact person.

United States Environmental Protection Agency (EPA)
Office of Water Policy
Washington, DC 20460
(202) 282-7818

CHAPTER III

Lifelong Learning

≋

"Education is the best provision for old age."
ARISTOTLE

The joy of learning is a natural motivator for growth. It makes an infant reach for a rattle and puts men on the moon. Though the ability to learn normally remains constant until at least age seventy, our childhood curiosity is often stifled along the way to adulthood. School, rather than providing an environment for the natural expression of our curiosity, often became a place where our true natures were regimented, shaped, and controlled in preparation for the workplace. Except for a few limited "elective" subjects, we followed a prescribed course of study, after which many of us lost a taste for the pursuit of knowledge.

Retirement gives you the chance to look at the world anew, and like a child, satisfy your enthusiasm for learning. You may explore anything you wish, for no other reason than you are interested. You need not prepare yourself for employment unless you want to. You don't have to work toward a degree unless you want one. You don't even have to take any tests if you don't want to. The only criteria you need to follow is how satisfying the learning experience is for you.

Maybe you wanted to explore a subject but financial or family responsibilities kept you from it. You can pursue it now, no matter how impractical it may be. Maybe you never had the chance to finish high school or get the degree you wanted. Now you can. Maybe there have been new developments in your field that you would like to catch up with or maybe there is something you're good at but haven't had the time to perfect.

There are many reasons to continue learning. Keeping the mind stimulated is the best way to retain intellectual ability. Not exercising your mind can lead to deterioration and loss of mental capacity. Education keeps your mind vital and active. It brings you into contact with interesting people and ideas and provides opportunities for challenge and accomplishment. You can earn an academic degree, gain a practical skill, or learn a hobby. Studying philosophy, religion, literature, language, or art can broaden your outlook and provide a continued sense of purpose. Physical education, health care, business, and home economics courses can prepare you for new job skills or voluntary service.

Learning is a process that continues throughout life. It is not limited to classrooms or the early years. The notion that education is just for kids has long since passed. The myth that our capacity to learn decreases with age dies hard, but research has proven that we continually learn through life, building on our life experiences and accumulated knowledge. Many educators believe older learners make better students. Since they can freely choose their course of study, they are keenly interested in learning and more disciplined. The presence of older learners in classrooms actually enriches the learning process for younger students, giving discussions added dimension and perspective from voices with real-life experience.

Ann Jaffe, a former art teacher for New York City, was always a creative person, but until she retired her creativity was directed outward, in assisting her students and family. Once she retired she was able to focus on the things that interested her and explore her creativity without thought to practical application. First, she took continuing education classes at New York University in drama, art, and anthropology, just because they were fun. Then she began to direct her energies into jewelry making. She had always enjoyed working with metal, but when her hands weakened she turned to beads. Studying the history of beads and their use by different cultures brought her to Mexico, where she studied jewelry at St. Megell University. A member of the Institute of Retired Professionals at the New School for Social Research, she was encouraged to use her skills to teach others. She now teaches her peers the art of beads at the IRP. She has also started her own home industry exhibiting and selling her beadwork at various art shows. Ann is a fine example of how education can lead to a lifetime of activity. Now in her late seventies, she is as involved and stimulated by life as ever. Her interest in education remains active. She has recently become interested in computers and plans to take a course to become computer literate.

Though age does not decrease our capacity to learn, it does change the ways and reasons we learn. After an absence of twenty or thirty years from the classroom, it may take a while getting the gears of learning lubricated again. By following the advice given to high school and elementary students you can get into the swing in no time. Just follow these simple ground rules:

- Don't try to absorb an entire subject at once. Break the material into small sections and learn a little at a time.
- Work at an easy pace. Take breaks.

- Establish a comfortable study area where you won't be disturbed.
- Pick a study time when your mind is active and free from distractions.
- Establish a regular study schedule and keep to that time.
- Don't strain your eyes. Read by a good light and select large-print books whenever possible.

Whether you want to go to college for an advanced degree or take a short course on quilting, there are a wealth of programs to choose from. You need not even leave the confines of you own home: telecourses and correspondence courses are available. If you are interested in the exchange of ideas, you can join a discussion group at your local library or museum. Your neighborhood high school probably runs continuing-education programs, as do the YMCA and religious organizations. Many colleges and universities, looking to fill the spaces left by the now-grown baby-boomers, have special programs for older adults. In some cases, arrangements can be made to audit classes on a space-available basis free of charge. You can even combine the fun of travel with the joy of learning and take a learning vacation.

High schools, colleges, YMCAs, and community centers all offer an array of noncredit classes for the adult learner in their continuing-education programs, ranging in subjects from technical skills to high school equivalency to hobbies. Most classes are held in the evening and discounts for older students are often available. Contact your local school board or high school for information. The library is also an excellent place to look for information on educational resources. There are many reference guides to colleges, universities and continuing-education programs. Most libraries keep a community bulletin board with information on lectures, discussion groups, and local programs.

Your state's director of adult education can supply you with information about basic and continuing education programs in your community.

STATE DIRECTORS OF ADULT EDUCATION

ALABAMA
Coordinator, ABE Section
Gordon Persons Bldg.,
  Rm. 5343
50 North Ripley Street
Montgomery, AL 36130
(205) 242-8181

ALASKA
Director, Adult & Voc/Ed
Alaska Department of
  Education
Box F
Juneau, AK 99811
(907) 465-4685

ARIZONA
Director, Adult Education
State Department of Education
1535 West Jefferson Street
Phoenix, AZ 85007
(602) 542-5281

ARKANSAS
Director, Adult Education
  Section
Voc/Tech Education Division
Department of Education

2020 W. 3rd
Executive Bldg. Suite 620
Little Rock, AR 72205
(501) 371-2263

CALIFORNIA
State Director
Adult Education
Department of Education
PO Box 944272
Sacramento, CA 94244-2720
(916) 322-2175

COLORADO
State Director, ABE
Division of Adult Education
State Dept. of Education
21 E. Colfax Avenue
Denver, CO 80203
(303) 866-6611

CONNECTICUT
Director, Division of Voc/Tech
  & Adult Education
Department of Education
25 Industrial Park Road
Middletown, CT 06457
(203) 638-4035

DELAWARE
State Supervisor
Adult/Community Education
PO Box 1402
J.G. Townsend Building
Dover, DE 19901
(302) 736-4668

DISTRICT OF COLUMBIA
District of Columbia Public
  Schools
Browne Administrative Unit
26th & Benning Rd., N.E.
Washington, D.C. 20002
(202) 724-4178

FLORIDA
Chief, Bureau of Adult/
  Community Education
Knott Building
Tallahassee, FL 32301
(904) 487-4929

GEORGIA
Commissioner for Adult
  Literacy
Department of Tech. & A.E.
660 South Tower
One CNN Center
Atlanta, GA 30303-2705
(404) 656-5845

HAWAII
Administrator, Youth & Early
  Childhood Section
Department of Education
c/o Hahaione Elementary
  School
595 Pepeekeo Street, H-2
Honolulu, HI 96825
(808) 395-9451

IDAHO
Director, Adult Education
Department of Education
Len B. Jordon Office Bldg.
650 W. State Street
Boise, ID 83720
(208) 334-2187

ILLINOIS
Director, Adult Education
Adult, Voc/Tech Education
Illinois State Board of Educ.
100 N. First Street–E-439
Springfield, IL 62777
(217) 782-3370

INDIANA
Director, Division of Adult &
  Community Education
Room 229, Statehouse
Indianapolis, IN 46204
(317) 232-0522

IOWA
Chief, Adult Education
Department of Education
Grimes State Office Bldg.
Des Moines, IA 50319-0146
(515) 281-3671

KANSAS
Director, Adult Education
Department of Education
120 East 10th Street
Topeka, KS 66612
(913) 296-3191

KENTUCKY
Director
Adult Education Division
Office of Federal Programs
State Dept. of Education
Frankfort, KY 40601
(502) 564-3921

LOUISIANA
Director, Adult Education
Louisiana Department of
  Education
PO Box 44064, Capitol
  Station
Baton Rouge, LA 70804
(504) 342-3510

MAINE
Director, Division of Adult &
  Community Education

State House Station–No. 23
Augusta, ME 04333
(207) 289-5854

MARYLAND
Director
Adult & Community
  Education Branch
Maryland State Department
  of Education
200 West Baltimore Street
Baltimore, MD 21201
(301) 333-2361

MASSACHUSETTS
Director
Bureau of Adult Services
Massachusetts Department of
  Education
Quincy Center Plaza
1385 Hancock Street
Quincy, MA 02169
(617) 770-7581

MICHIGAN
Director
Adult Extended Learning
  Services
Michigan Department of
  Education
PO Box 30008
Lansing, MI 48909
(517) 373-8425

MINNESOTA
Coordinator
Adult Basic Education
997 Capitol Square Building
550 Cedar Street
St. Paul, MN 55101
(612) 296-6130

MISSISSIPPI
Branch Director II
Division of Adult Education
State Department of
  Education
PO Box 771
Jackson, MS 39205
(601) 359-3464

MISSOURI
Director, Adult Education
Department of Elementary
  and Secondary Education
213 Adams Street, PO Box
  480
Jefferson City, MO 65102
(314) 751-0887

MONTANA
Director, Adult Education
Office of the State
  Superintendent
State Capitol Building
Helena, MT 59620
(406) 444-4443

NEBRASKA
Director, Adult & Community
  Education
Nebraska Department of
  Education
301 Centennial Mall South
PO Box 94987
Lincoln, NE 68509
(402) 471-4807

NEVADA
State Supervisor, ABE
State Department of
  Education
400 W. King Street
Carson City, NV 89710
(702) 885-3133

NEW HAMPSHIRE
Supervisor, ABE
Department of Education
101 Pleasant Street
Concord, NH 03301
(603) 271-2247

NEW JERSEY
Director, Adult Education
Dept. of Education
225 West State Street
Trenton, NJ 08625-0500
(609) 777-1462

NEW MEXICO
State Director, ABE
Department of Education
Education Building
300 Don Gaspar
Santa Fe, NM 87501
(505) 827-6675

NEW YORK
Director, Division of
   Continuing Education
State Education Department
Washington Avenue
Albany, NY 12234
(518) 474-5808

NORTH CAROLINA
Director, Continuing
   Education
Department of Community
   Colleges
200 West Jones
Raleigh, NC 27063-1337
(919) 733-4791

NORTH DAKOTA
Director, Adult Education
Department of Public
   Instruction
9th Floor, State Capitol Bldg.
Bismarck, ND 58505
(701) 224-2393 or 224-4567

OHIO
Director
Division of Educational
   Services
65 S. Front Street–Rm. 811
Columbus, OH 43212
(614) 466-4962

OKLAHOMA
Administrator, Adult
   Education Section
Department of Education
Oliver Hodge Memorial
   Education Bldg.
2500 N. Lincoln Blvd.–
   Rm. 180
Oklahoma City, OK 73105
(405) 521-3321

OREGON
Director
Community College Instruction
   Service
Office of Community Colleges
700 Pringle Parkway
Salem, OR 97310
(503) 378-8585

PENNSYLVANIA
Division of Adult Basic &
   Literacy Education Program
Bureau of Voc/Adult
   Education
Department of Education

333 Market Street, 6th Floor
Harrisburg, PA 17126-0333
(717) 787-5532

RHODE ISLAND
Adult Education
Department of Education
22 Hayes Street, Room 222
Roger Williams Building
Providence, RI 02908
(401) 277-2705

SOUTH CAROLINA
Director, Adult Education
Department of Education
Rutledge Building, Room 209
1429 Senate Street
Columbia, SC 29201
(803) 734-8070

SOUTH DAKOTA
Division of Elementary &
  Secondary Education
KNEIP Building
Pierre, SD 57501
(605) 773-4716

TENNESSEE
Executive Director
Division of Adult &
  Community Education
Department of Education
1130 Menzler Road
Nashville, TN 37210
(615) 741-7054

TEXAS
Program Director, Adult
  Education
Division of Adult Education/
  Employment Training,
  Funding & Compliance
Texas Education Agency
1701 North Congress Avenue
Austin, TX 78701
(512) 463-9294

UTAH
Adult Education Services
Office of Education
25 East 5th Street South
Salt Lake City, UT 84111
(801) 538-7844

VERMONT
Chief, Adult Education Unit
State Office Building
Montpelier, VT 05602
(802) 828-3131

VIRGINIA
Director, Adult Education
Department of Education
Commonwealth of Virginia
PO Box 6Q
Richmond, VA 23216
(804) 225-2075

WASHINGTON
Director, Adult Education
Community/Interagency
  Services
Old Capitol Building
Olympia, WA 98504
(206) 753-6748

WEST VIRGINIA
Director, Adult Education
Department of Education
Building 6, Unit B-230
State Capitol Complex
19 Washington Street East
Charleston, WV 25305
(304) 348-6318

WISCONSIN
Adult Basic Education
  Consultant
Wisconsin Board of Voc/Tech
  and Adult Education
310 Price Place
PO Box 7874
Madison, WI 53707
(608) 267-9684

WYOMING
Coordinator, Adult Education
Department of Education
Hathaway Building
Cheyenne, WY 82002
(307) 777-6228

AMERICAN SAMOA
Dean of Continuing and
  Adult Education
American Samoa Community
  College
Board of Higher Education
Mapusaga Campus
PO Box 2609
Pago Pago, American Samoa
  96799
(684) 699-9155

GUAM
Director, Division of Career
  and Public Service
Guam Community College
PO Box 23069
Main Postal Facility
Guam, MI 96921
(671) 734-4311

NORTHERN MARIANA
  ISLANDS
Director, Adult Basic
  Education
Northern Marianas College
Commonwealth of the
  Northern Mariana Islands
Saipan, MI 96950
(670) 234-6171

PUERTO RICO
Assistant Secretary for Adult
  Education

Department of Education
PO Box 759
Hato Rey, PR 00919
(809) 753-9211

REPUBLIC OF PALAU
Director of Education
Office of Ministry of Social
  Services
Republic of Palau
PO Box 189
Koror, Palau 96940
Int. Oper. 160-680-952

VIRGIN ISLANDS
Director, Adult Education
Department of Education
PO Box 6640
St. Thomas, VI 00801
(809) 774-5394

INSTITUTE OF LIFETIME LEARNING AARP

The American Association of Retired Persons maintains a resource center on education for older people. The Institute of Lifetime Learning promotes learning opportunities for older people and encourages volunteerism in schools and literacy programs. Serving as a national clearinghouse on continuing education for older people, it offers free study materials and information booklets, and provides technical help to organizations and institutions interested in developing educational programs for older learners.

Institute of Lifetime Learning
American Association of Retired Persons
Program Department
601 E Street NW
Washington, DC 20049

For their excellent resource, "Learning Opportunities for Older Persons," Publication D171, a guide to the many options for continuing education including colleges, universities, correspondence courses, learning vacations, and self-planned programs, write:

AARP Fulfillment
601 E Street NW
Washington, DC 20049

BASIC EDUCATION

For many people, retirement is the first opportunity they have to learn how to read, write, or speak English. More than 23 million Americans are classified as functionally illiterate. Of this group, 44 percent are over the age of fifty, with people sixty years and older comprising a third of the total illiterate population. There are many reasons for adult illiteracy. Growing up during wartime or the Depression forced many people to leave school and get a job to help support their families. Others grew up on farms where every member of the family was needed to work. Many people moved around a lot, jumping from one school to the next, and others had illiterate parents and received poor early education. Others lost the skills they once had due to lack of use. Consequently, many people lack the basic skills most of us take for granted, like reading a menu, writing a check, or filling out a Social Security application.

Most people who manage to get through life with limited skills learn to compensate through tricks such as memorizing, telling white lies (I left my glasses at home) and having their family and friends help them. Though these means may get one by, they are no solution and the pain and embarrassment of not knowing what you think you should by now has a lasting effect. Life changes—such as living on a fixed income, loss of a spouse, and increased leisure time—make the need for basic skills even greater. Though it is difficult to step forward and admit such a lack in later life, for those who do the rewards of learning are great.

Imagine the joy of a grandfather who can, for the first time, read the letters his grandchildren send, or the pride of a widow who can now manage her own checkbook.

In 1983, the federal government recognized the need for providing basic education to adults and established the Adult Literacy Initiative to coordinate efforts between the public and private sectors. Many organizations are involved in the fight against illiteracy, including the American Library Association, AARP, National Issues Forums, and Literacy Volunteers. To locate a basic adult education program in your area call toll free:

National Literacy Hotline
(800) 228-8813

High School Equivalency

If you have not completed your high school education, you are far from alone. Seventy percent of adults over fifty-five have not finished high school. Yet every year, thousands of Americans prove it is never too late to learn. Ruth Story received her high school diploma through home study at the age of eighty-six. She had begun her studies fifteen years before but, due to illness in the family, was not able to finish. Knowing she was only a few credits away from her degree, she approached the school to see if they still had her records. They did and awarded her a high school diploma based on a demonstration of her communication skills. "I learned a lot and got a great deal of self-satisfaction after finally becoming a high school graduate and wear my class ring proudly." At age seventy-one, Richard Anthony Dickenson of Largo, Florida, was tired of being put down for his lack of high school education and decided to do something about it, as did Joe Morrane, seventy-four, of Philadelphia, Pennsylvania. Both obtained their high school equivalency through the General Educational Development (GED) examination.

The GED is a five-part examination that tests your skills in writing, social studies, science, reading, and mathematics. The test is sponsored by the American Council on Education and is accepted by almost all colleges and employers as equivalent to a traditional high school diploma. Nearly every community offers courses to help you prepare for the GED. Teachers are skilled in assisting adults to overcome their fears and insecurities about returning to school late in life. Often the education you picked up on your own through reading or life experience is preparation in itself for the test. Study guides are available in most bookstores, and public-television stations provide instructional programming.

Contact your local school board for information, or write:

GED Testing Service
One Dupont Circle
Washington, DC 20036-1163
(202) 939-9490

COLLEGE PROGRAMS

Retirement is an excellent time to obtain a college degree, an advanced degree, or to attend classes for the pure joy of learning. Today, college students can be any age. Irving Weiner, 68, a retired vice chairman of a Houston department store, studies at the University of Houston Law Center. He plans to get a degree in geriatric law. Colleges and universities offer many different kinds of learning opportunities for older adults. College Centers for Older Learners provide peer-learning environments where you can enjoy the self-enrichment of study without the pressure of working toward a degree. Many schools have special arrangements for older adults to audit courses on a space-available basis free of charge, giving you the option of intergenerational learning side-by-side with today's college students. For information on what colleges offer reduced or free tuition, contact your state office of higher education or individual schools directly. It is also possible to obtain college credit for life experience or receive credit for off-campus learning and independent study.

Before selecting a school or course of study, visit the campus. Check out the proximity to transportation. See if there are places to read, a library, cafeteria, or recreational facilities. Look over their brochure. Talk to the faculty and other students. Find out what portion of the fees will be returned if the course is not to your liking.

Older students wishing to complete a degree may be eligible for reduced tuition or scholarship assistance; contact the school's financial-aid office. Other resources for information on financial aid are available at your public library:

The Annual Register of Grant Support (Los Angeles, CA: Marquis Academic Media, updated annually)

Grants Register (New York, NY: Martins Press, updated biennially)

A booklet, "The Student Guide: Five Federal Programs," is available free of charge from the Federal Student Aid Program, PO Box 84, Washington, DC 20044.

COLLEGE-LEVEL EXAMINATION PROGRAM (CLEP)

You may be eligible for college credits for what you already know. Knowledge accumulated through life experience, on the job, and from volunteer work, earlier studies, reading, and independent study can be turned into academic credit through the College-Level Examination Program. A sixty-five-year-old widow found that her volunteer work in community projects was worth seventeen sociology credits. A retired businessman received twenty-six credits in marketing for his knowledge and a couple in their late 50s earned fifteen credits each for their work on environmental-protection projects.

Nearly three-quarters of all accredited institutions of higher education accept satisfactory scores on CLEP examinations as credit. You may be able to enter or re-enter college with up to two full years of college credit, allowing you to bypass introductory-level courses in subjects you already know and go directly to more challenging and satisfying material. For those reluctant to start or return to college after many years of being out of the classroom, CLEP provides a concrete way to compare your performance with college-level achievement and increase your confidence in your ability to compete academically. It can also improve your chances for acceptance at the college of your choice by providing the admissions department with up-to-date information on your academic skills.

Exams in five general areas measure proficiency in the material covered by the liberal-arts courses required during the first two years of college. They include English composition, humanities, mathematics, natural sciences, and history. Subject examinations that measure knowledge in specific areas are available in thirty different subjects. CLEP examinations are available each month at more than twelve hundred test centers across the country.

For a free booklet and listing of institutions awarding credit through CLEP examinations and locations where CLEP tests are administered, write to:

"Make Learning Pay"
CLEP Box 6600
Department Examinations
Princeton, NJ 08541
(215) 750-8420

UNIVERSITIES WITHOUT WALLS

If you have the ability to learn on your own, you can obtain a college degree without entering a classroom. Several institutions grant associate, bachelors, masters, and doctoral degrees through independent-study programs, correspondence courses, and life-experience credit. Some provide structured learning materials or take advantage of modern technology using computers, television, or video-cassette recorders. Others will let you design your own program under the guidance of a faculty advisor. Some require full-time commitment while others allow part-time study at your own pace. The following institutions offering external degree programs are accredited by the National Home Study Council.

Ohio University
External Student Program
309 Tupper Hall
Athens, OH 45701
(800) 444-2420

Regents College of the
  University of the State
  of New York
Cultural Education Center
Albany, NY 12230
(518) 474-3703

The Union Institute
Undergraduate Studies
Suite 1010
632 Vine Street
Cincinnati, OH 45202
(513) 621-6444

American Open University of
  New York
Institute of Technology
Building 66, Office 227
Central Islip, NY 11722
(516) 348-3000

Center for Distance Learning
Empire State College
2 Union Avenue
Saratoga Springs, NY 12866
(518) 587-2100

Goddard College
Plainfield, VT 05667
(802) 454-8311

Thomas A. Edison State
  College
101 West State Street
Trenton, NJ 08625
(609) 984-1100

For further information on alternative and external degree programs, contact:

Council for Adult
  and Experiential Learning
National Headquarters
Suite 510
226 West Jackson
Chicago, Illinois 60606
(312) 922-5909

American Council on Education
Center for Adult Learning
  and Educational Credentials
External Degree Guide and
  Conference Series
One Dupont Circle
Washington, DC 20036-1193
(202) 939-9407

National Home Study Council
1601 Eighteenth Street NW
Washington, DC 20009
(202) 234-5100

COLLEGE CENTERS FOR OLDER LEARNERS

Colleges and universities recognize the potential of older learners and are offering special programs to meet their unique needs and interests. Programs designed exclusively for older learners offer a relaxed environment, free from the pressure of grades and tests, where you can pursue individual educational goals while enjoying an exchange of ideas and social activities with your peers.

Some programs are academically oriented. Others focus on practical or recreational subjects and some combine both. Many programs are student directed, involving students in academic decisions. Often classes are taught by retired people drawn from the student body, with students acting as resource people or discussion leaders. School-directed programs, planned by the continuing-education department of the school, may be taught by paid instructors with input by the students on course selection. Many programs include the use of college facilities, such as the library, cafeteria, or recreation areas. Opportunities to participate in the cultural life of the college, including films, concerts, plays, and lectures are generally available, as are group activities such as tours, luncheons, and discussions. Most programs have no entrance requirements. Many of the participants never attended college before. Programs geared specifically to retired professionals may require committee review for acceptance. Fees range from nothing to several hundred dollars a semester.

The following by-state listing of College Centers for Older Learners was provided by AARP and Elderhostel Institute Network. Many more are opening all the time. Contact your local university or college for the College Center nearest you.

Alabama
Prime Life Program
Athens State College
Athens, AL 35611
(202) 232-1802

Auburn University
Academy for Lifelong Learners
100 Mell Hall
Auburn, AL 36849-5610
(205) 944-3102

Senior University
Auburn University at
  Montgomery
Division of Continuing
  Education
Montgomery, AL 36117
(205) 244-3341

Alaska
Tanana Valley Community
  College
4280 Geist Road
Fairbanks, AK 99701
(907) 456-8822

Arizona
Senior Adult Program
Phoenix College
1202 West Thomas Road
Phoenix, AZ 85013
(602) 624-2492

Senior Education Program
Pima Community College
200 North Stone Avenue
Tucson, AZ 85701
(602) 884-6060

California
Modesto Junior College
College Avenue
Modesto, CA 95350-9977
(209) 575-6067

College of the Emeritus
San Diego Community College
1400 Park Boulevard
San Diego, CA 92101
(619) 230-2039

Educational Growth
  Opportunities
San Diego State University
San Diego, CA 92182
(619) 265-5384

Santa Monica Community
  College
1900 Pico Boulevard
Santa Monica, CA 90405
(213) 450-5150

Plato Society
University of California at Los
  Angeles
Extension Division
10995 LeConte Avenue
Los Angeles, CA 90024
(213) 743-4343

Institute for Continued
  Learning
University of California at San
  Diego
University Extension Q-014
LaJolla, CA 92093
(714) 452-3409

Center for Learning in
  Retirement
University of California at San
  Francisco
Extension Center
55 Laguna Street
San Francisco, CA 04102
(415) 863-4518

The Fromm Institute for
  Lifelong Learning
University of San Francisco
2130 Fulton Street
San Francisco, CA 04117
(415) 666-6805

Colorado
Learning Throughout Life
Amis Community College
PO Box 69
Greeley, CO 80632
(303) 330-8008

Emeritus College
Arapahoe Community College
5900 South Santa Fe Drive
Littleton, CA 80120
(303) 797-5621

Lifelong Learning Center
Pueblo Community College
900 West Orman
Pueblo, CO 81004
(303) 549-3372

Connecticut
University of the Third Age
Asnuntuck Community College
PO Box 68
170 Elm Street
Enfield, CT 06082
(203) 754-1603

Retired Professional Institute
Fairfield University
North Benson Road
Fairfield, CT 06430
(203) 255-5411

ALP (Adult Learning
   Program)
Hartford Consortium for
   Higher Education
260 Girard Avenue
Hartford, CT 06105
(203) 236-1203

Institute for Learning in
   Retirement
University of Connecticut
The Bishop Center, Box U13
Storres, CT 06269
(203) 486-5383

Community Interest Program
Saint Joseph College
1678 Asylum Avenue
West Hartford, CT 06117
(203) 232-4571

Delaware
Graying of the Campus
Education for Older Adults
Delaware State College
Center for Continuing
   Education
Dover, DE 19901
(302) 736-5143

Academy of Lifelong Learning
University of Delaware
Wilcastle Center
2800 Pennsylvania Avenue
Wilmington, DE 19806
(203) 738-8154

District of Columbia
Institute for Learning in
   Retirement
The American University
Nebraska Hall
4400 Massachusetts Avenue
   NW
Washington, DC 20016
(202) 885-3920

Continuing Education for
Older Adults Program
University of the District of
Columbia
Institute of Gerontology
Room 114
1100 Harvard Street NW
Washington, DC 20009

Florida
Institute for Retired
Professionals
University of Miami
Allen Hall, PO Box 248005
Coral Gables, FL 33124
(305) 284-2222

Academy of Senior
Professionals
Eckerd College
PO Box 12560
St. Petersburg, FL 33712
(813) 866-2671

Manatee Community College
5840 26th Street West
PO Box 1849
Bradenton, FL 33507
(813) 755-1511

Institute for Retired
Professionals
Nova University
3301 College Avenue
Fort Lauderdale, FL 33143
(305) 475-7336

The Institute of New
Dimensions
Palm Beach Junior College
4200 Congress Avenue
Lake Worth, FL 33461
(305) 439-8106

PJC Seniors Club
Pensacola Junior College
1000 College Boulevard
Pensacola, FL 32504
(904) 476-5410

Institute of Lifetime Learning
Valencia Community College
PO Box 3028
Orlando, FL 32802
(305) 299-5000

Illinois
Lifelong Learners Club
Parkland College
2400 West Bradley Avenue
Champaign, IL 61821
(217) 351-2200

Institute of Lifetime Learning
Southern Illinois University at
Edwardville
Box 84
University of Edwardville
Edwardville, IL 62026
(618) 692-3210

Institute for Learning in
  Retirement
Northwestern University
Anderson Hall
2003 Sheriden Road
Evanston, IL 60201
(708) 491-3741

Indiana
Gerontology Program
Vincennes University
1002 North First Street
Vincennes, IN 47591
(812) 885-4119

Iowa
Chautaugua Program for
  Senior Adults
Cornell College
Mount Vernon, IA 52314
(319) 895-8811

Kansas
Bethel College
North Newton, KS 67117
(316) 283-2500

Life Enrichment
Butler County Community
  College
901 S. Haverhill Road
Eldorado, KS 67042
(316) 321-5083

Xtra Years of Zest (XYZ)
Cowley County Community
  College
125 South 2nd Street
Arkansas City, KS 67005
(316) 442-0430

Tabor College
400 South Jefferson
Hillsboro, KS 67073
(316) 947-3121

University of Kansas
Lawrence, KS 66045
(913) 864-2700

Washburn Walkers
University of Topeka
17th and College
Topeka, KS 66621
(913) 295-6300

Louisiana
Senior Adult Education
Centenary College of Louisiana
PO Box 4188
Shreveport, LA 71134
(318) 869-5115

Maryland
Life
Anne Arundel Community
  College
101 College Parkway
Arnold, MD 21012
(301) 269-4561

Johns Hopkins University
Charles and 34th Streets
Baltimore, MD 21218
(301) 338-8000

Institute for Retired Persons
Salisbury State College
College and Camden Avenues
Salisbury, MD 21801
(301) 543-6170

Massachusetts
Seniors for Lifelong Learning
Curry College
Milton, MA 02186
(617) 333-0500

Institute for Learning in
  Retirement
Harvard University
Lehman Hall, B-3
Cambridge, MA 02138
(617) 495-1000

Lifelong Learning
Northern Essex Community
  College
100 Elliott Street
Haverhill, MA 01830
(617) 374-0721

Five College Learning in
  Retirement
University of Massachusetts,
  Amherst
Goodell Hall
Amherst, MA 01002
(413) 545-0111

Learning in Retirement
  Association
University of Lowell
One University Center
Lowell, MA 01854
(508) 934-2936

Learning in Later Life
Springfield College
PO Box 1793
Springfield, MA 01109
(413) 788-3000

Center for Creative Aging
Endicott College
Beverly, MA 01915
(508) 927-0585

Academy for Lifelong
  Learning
Center for Successful Aging
Cape Cod Community College
West Barnstable, MA 02668
(508) 362-2131

Michigan
Emeritus Institute
Aquinas College
1607 Robinson Road
Grand Rapids, MI 49506
(616) 459-8281

Hope Academy of Senior
    Professionals
Hope College
Holland, MI 49423
(616) 392-5111

Learning in Retirement
University of Michigan
Turner Geriatric Services
1010 Wall Street
Ann Arbor, MI 48109
(313) 764-1817

New Hampshire
Active Retired Association
University of New Hampshire
Durham, NH 03824
(603) 862-1088

New Jersey
Educational Programs for
    Older Persons
Fairleigh Dickinson University
285 Madison Avenue
Madison, NJ 07940
(201) 593-8500

Montclair State College
Upper Montclair, NJ 07043
(201) 893-4000

New York
Adelphi University
Garden City, NY 11530
(516) 294-8700

Institute for Retired
    Professionals and Executives
Brooklyn College of the City
    of New York
Bedford Avenue and
    Avenue H
Brooklyn, NY 11210
(718) 780-5044

College Emeritus
College of Mount Saint Vincent
Riverdale, NY 10471
(212) 549-1120

College at 60
Fordham University at
    Lincoln Center
113 West 60th Street
Room 806
New York, NY 10023
(212) 841-5334

Professionals and Executives in Retirement (PEIR)
Hofstra University
Room 018, Weller Hall
1000 Hempstead Turnpike
Hempstead, NY 11550
(516) 560-6744

My Turn Program
Kingsborough Community College
Oriental Boulevard
Brooklyn, NY 11235
(718) 934-5079

Learning in Retirement
Nazareth College of Rochester
4245 East Avenue
Rochester, NY 14610
(716) 586-2525

Institute for Retired Professionals
New School for Social Research
66 W. 12th Street
New York, NY 10011
(212) 741-5682

Institute of Study for Older Adults
New York City Technical College

Division of Continuing Education
800 Jay Street
Brooklyn, NY 11201
(718) 643-4900

Active Retired Center
Pace University
1 Peace Plaza
New York, NY 10038
(212) 488-1288

Institute for Senior Education
Rockland Community College
145 College Road
Suffern, NY 10901
(914) 356-4650

Studies for Mature Adults
Skidmore College
Saratoga Springs, NY 12866
(518) 584-5000

Institute for Retired Professionals
Syracuse University
Syracuse, NY 13202
(315) 423-3250

Mainstream, The Retirement Institute
Westchester Community College
75 Grasslands Road
Valhalla, NY 10595
(914) 285-6793

Academy for Lifelong
  Learning
Union College
Wells House, 1 Union Avenue
Schenectady, NY 12300
(518) 370-6000

LYCEUM
School of Education and
  Human Development
State University of New York,
  Binghamton
Binghamton, NY 13901
(607) 777-2000

North Carolina
Bennett College
900 East Washington Street
Greensboro, NC 27401-3239
(919) 273-4431

Duke Institute for Learning
Duke University
Office of Continuing Education
The Bishop's House
Durham, NC 27708
(919) 684-6259

Saturday School for Senior
  Citizens
Durham Technical Institute
410 Caldwell Street
Chapel Hill, NC 27514
(919) 958-4478
Contact: Orange County
  Department on Aging

University of North Carolina
  at Greensboro
100 Spring Garden Street
Greensboro, NC 27412
(919) 379-5930

Learning Institute for Elders
  (LIFE)
Mars Hill College
Mars Hill, NC 28754
(704) 689-1166

Village Elders
University of North Carolina
Chapel Hill, NC 27514
(919) 962-2211

Ohio
Case Western Reserve
  University
University Circle
Cleveland, OH 44106
(216) 368-2000

Elders Program
Cuyahoga Community
  College
4250 Richmond Road
Warrensville Township, OH
  44122
(216) 469-9359

Ohio State University
Columbus, OH 43210-1358
(614) 422-6446

Institute for Learning in
   Retirement
University of Cincinnati
MP.L. 146, 350 French Hall
Cincinnati, OH 45221-0146
(513) 558-1000

Oregon
Retired Association of Portland
State University
Portland State University
PO Box 751
Portland, OR 92707
(503) 229-4739

Pennsylvania
Community Scholars Program
Beaver College
Glenside, PA 19038
(215) 572-2122

Institute for Learning in
   Retirement
Cedar Crest College
Allentown, PA 18104
(215) 437-4471

Keystone Junior College
La Plume, PA 18440
(717) 945-5141

Late Start Program
Northhampton County Area
   Community College
2945 Oakland Road
Bethlehem, PA 18017
(215) 861-5500

Association for Retired
   Professionals
Temple University, Center City
1616 Walnut Street
Philadelphia, PA 19103
(215) 787-1505

Rhode Island
Brown University
Providence, RI 02912
(401) 863-1000

Texas
Lifetime Learning Institute
PO Box 2285
Austin, TX 78749
(512) 452-7661

Adult Life and Learning
Brazosport College
500 College Drive
Lake Jackson, TX 77566
(409) 265-6131

Senior Citizens Educational Program
DelMar College
Baldwin at Ahers
Corpus Christi, TX 78404
(512) 881-6326

Center for Professional Development
East Texas State University at Texarkana
PO Box 5518
Texarkana, TX 75518
(214) 838-6514

Senior Avocational Vocation Education Program (SAVE)
Grayson County College
6101 Grayson Drive
Denison, TX 75020
(214) 465-6030

Houston Institute for Lifetime Learning
Houston Community College
Suite 112
3333 Fanvin
Houston, TX 77004
(713) 868-0723

Senior Adult Institute
Lee College
Bayton, TX 77520
(713) 425-6302

Center for Lifelong Learning
University of Texas, El Paso
Suite 108, Miner's Hall
El Paso, TX 79968-0602
(915) 747-5000

Virginia
Elderscholar
Roanoke College
Salem, VA 24153
(703) 389-2351

Free University for Senior Citizens
Virginia Commonwealth Free University
301 West Franklin Street
Richmond, VA 23220
(804) 786-0342

New Dimensions
Virginia Polytechnic Institute and State University
Blacksburg, VA 24061
(703) 961-6267

ElderLearning Society
Christopher Newport College
50 Shoe Lane
Newport News, VA 23606
(703) 594-7568

Washington
Focus on Mature Learning
Clark College
1800 East McLoughlin
  Boulevard
Vancouver, WA 98663
(206) 699-0358

Institute for Extended
  Learning
Spokane Falls Community
  College
West 3410 Fort George Wright
  Drive
Spokane, WA 99204-5288
(509) 459-3762

Wisconsin
Guild for Learning in
  Retirement
University of Wisconsin,
  Milwaukee
PO Box 749, Office of the
  Registrar
Milwaukee, WI 53201
(414) 963-7800

INSTITUTE FOR RETIRED PROFESSIONALS (IRP)

In 1962, a retired school teacher, Hyman Hirsh, approached the New School for Social Research in New York City with the novel idea of establishing a learning program for retired educators and executives. It was an instant success. The idea spread across the country and now many colleges and universities use the Institute for Retired Professionals model to establish similar programs. The institute's concept is involving older learners in developing their own educational community. This results in an atmosphere where adults expand and enhance their own educational development by sharing experience, talent, and skills with other self-motivated learners.

Membership in IRP entitles learners to two kinds of educational experiences. They may enroll in one regular New School course each semester and participate in peer-learning seminars that meet either weekly or biweekly and range in subject from literature, art, music, history, languages, psychology, and public affairs to writing, painting, and ceramics. These groups are led by members of IRP who design the course outline and act as discussion leaders. The leaders are not necessarily experts in the subject, but are learners themselves engaged in the learning process. Often, a background paper prepared by one of the participants is used as the basis of discussion. Classes without background papers rely on assigned texts or students' familiarity with news stories and feature articles. All groups draw heavily on the experience of the participants in forming the basis of discussion.

At IRP, social activities are as much a part of learning as classroom experience. Most study groups have a secretary who coordinates extracurricular activities and keeps in touch with members absent due to illness. Tickets to cultural events, including Broadway and off-Broadway shows, concerts, and dance programs, are available to members. Day excursions to out-of-town museums, gardens, and cultural attractions are planned each semester. Members are also entitled to full library privileges and use of the school's cafeteria. IRP publishes an annual review containing the poems, essays, short stories, illustrations, and photography of members. An annual art show exhibits the work of IRP's painters, sculptors, ceramists, collagists, and photographers. The IRP lounge features one-person shows that change from month to month, allowing artists to feature their work.

All members share the responsibility of maintaining the intellectual climate of the institute. Each member is expected to be both a student and teacher and participate in the organization, design, and format of the curriculum. The policies of the institute are formulated by a twelve-member council elected by the members and a director appointed by the New School. Standing committees include admissions, art show, curriculum, newsletter, orientation, *IRP Review*, social activities, and New School courses. Many IRP members take an active role in the coordination and administration of IRP programs through participation in committees and as program coordinators, paper givers, and group secretaries.

Membership in IRP is open to anyone recently retired from a professional or executive career. Admission to the program is based on successful completion of an application form and an interview with a committee member. A yearly membership fee entitles members to participate in all IRP activities.

Institute for Retired Professionals
New School for Social Research
66 West 12th Street
New York, NY 10011
(212) 741-5682

CENTER FOR CREATIVE RETIREMENT

The North Carolina Center for Creative Retirement, on the campus of the University of North Carolina in Asheville, is a national model of how retirees and their communities can mutually benefit one another. Established in response to a growing retirement population, the center offers a variety of programs in community leadership, retirement planning, peer learning and teaching, health promotion, and intergenerational education. It also operates a research institute to study retirement issues.

Senior Leadership Seminars prepare retirees for meaningful volunteer or entrepreneurial positions within the Asheville community. Through a self-assessment and life-review process, retirees discover their unique talents and leadership qualities. The history, politics, economy, and human resources of the community is explored through hands-on case studies. Working teams select an issue or agency to study and report their findings to the group. The effectiveness of this program was demonstrated when leadership alumni organized a Seniors-in-the-Schools volunteer program that provides tutors, career counselors, lecturers, and advisors to local schools.

The Retirement Wellness Center encourages responsibility for one's own health. A sixteen-hour wellness course focuses on diet, stress management, exercise, and positive attitudes to promote a healthy lifestyle. Graduates may become wellness ambassadors and serve as public speakers, program planners, and mentors helping their community and peers achieve a high level of wellness.

The College for Seniors offers a peer-learning environment where retirees can study liberal arts courses free from the pressures of grades and tests. Classes are taught both by the university faculty and by retirees; they cover art, history, literature, and world affairs.

Retirement Issues Forums focus on critical issues related to aging. In a series of public forums, experts from academia, business, government and civic organizations explore the issues that most affect retirees.

The Senior Academy for Intergenerational Learning taps the knowledge and expertise of retired professionals to serve as mentors, tutors, and counselors, helping undergraduates turn their classroom work into practical career preparation.

Adults fifty-five and over are welcome to join the North Carolina Center for Retirement. The only prerequisite is the desire to seek new information and experience the joy of learning. A modest membership fee is required. Financial assistance is available for eligible participants.

North Carolina Center for Creative Retirement (UNCA)
Asheville, NC 28804-3299
(704) 251-6140

The College at 60, Fordham University

The College at 60 is recognized nationally as a model for independent colleges. It provides a comfortable transition from the work world to the college campus for people long out of school. Students begin in small, credit-bearing seminars within a community of peers. These seminars, taught by Fordham faculty, cover such topics as history, philosophy, literature, and computers. After successful completion of four seminars, students may enter Fordham's College of Liberal Arts, interacting with younger students in the full college curriculum.

This program is open to adults over fifty capable of college-level work. Many participants hold college degrees. Others are completing or beginning work toward bachelor's degrees. Classes are held during the day. Tuition, governed by the prevailing per-credit rate of the College at Lincoln Center, includes use of Fordham's library and facilities, the College at 60 lecture series, the student association, and student newspaper.

The College at 60
Room 422
The College at Lincoln Center
Fordham University
113 West 60th Street
New York, NY 10023
(212) 841-5334

OLDER ADULT SERVICE AND INFORMATION SYSTEM (OASIS)

OASIS is a unique concept in adult learning that combines the resources of the private and public sector to enrich the lives of people over age 55. The May Company, which owns department stores in 21 cities, provides permanently designated centers, including lounge and classroom space, while local hospitals and not-for-profit agencies sponsor programs.

The familiar and stimulating environment of department stores make excellent meeting places where active older adults can participate in educational, cultural, and social events. Classes are offered on such subjects as visual arts, music, drama, creative writing, contemporary issues, history, science, and health. OASIS members may also train to become volunteers and work as peer leaders in classrooms and intergenerational programs, serve as ushers at local theaters or help with the operations of OASIS centers.

To locate an OASIS center near you, look in your telephone book or contact the national headquarters:

OASIS
7710 Carondelect Avenue
Suite 125
St. Louis, MO 63105
(314) 862-2933

HOME STUDY

If learning by correspondence brings to mind matchbook-cover advertising and fly-by-night schools, look again. Home study can be a respectable, effective, moderately priced alternative to traditional education offering the kind of flexibility many of us require. It is widely recognized by educational institutions and private businesses alike as a way for highly motivated, self-directed individuals to increase their knowledge and improve their skills. Currently, more than 4 million Americans are enrolled in some type of home-study program.

Home study is especially attractive to retirees who wish to realize their educational goals at home, at their own pace. You can learn a new hobby, start a small business, enhance your voluntary-work skills, test your aptitude for a subject, get your high school diploma or college degree, or pursue self-fulfilling interests by letting the school come to you. The limitations that prevented you from realizing your educational potential (lack of a high school degree, lack of time, lack of money, geographical limitations, or fear of testing new ground) are no longer barriers.

Charles Roy Canster got his high school diploma through home study at the age of eighty-one. Frances Graham, a retired registered nurse, uses the skills she learned through a home-study sewing and design course to make dresses and suits for herself, her children, and her grandchildren. In preparation for retirement, Jack Allen of Fort Smith, Arizona, studied writing at home. He plans to write for profit after retiring.

Of the many changes in home-study programs in recent years, the most significant is in the quality of learning materials. Teaching by mail has become a science. Learning modules, which break down the material into understandable bits, allow the student to master one skill at a time. Modern technology offers a variety of learning methods, including audio, video, and computer-based materials. Prepared sequential lessons are sent to the student by mail. After completing each lesson, the student returns the assigned work to the institution for correction and evaluation by qualified instructors. A personalized student-teacher relationship is established through this exchange.

Before signing up for a course, make sure it meets your educational goals. If you are seeking college credit to apply toward a degree, check with the admissions office of the college you'd like to attend to be sure credits are transferable. If you are seeking licensing or a certificate in a particular field, contact the licensing authority to determine which courses fulfill the requirements. Carefully consider the information sent by the school and *ask questions*. What does the course cover? What materials are supplied? What are the credentials of the faculty members? What are the procedures for obtaining a professor's assistance? How much time do you have to complete the course? What is the school's refund policy? Be sure to read and understand your contract before signing it.

You can research a school's credibility by checking with the Better Business Bureau, the Office of Educational Credit and Credentials of the American Council of Education (One Dupont Circle, Washington, DC 20036), and the National Home Study Council.

THE NATIONAL HOME STUDY COUNCIL (NHSC)

The National Home Study Council is an independent non-profit organization that acts as an advocate and information clearinghouse for home study. It also sponsors an accrediting commission that evaluates home-study schools. Accreditation is granted to schools that have the following:

- A competent faculty
- Educationally sound and up-to-date courses
- Careful screening of students before admission
- Satisfactory record of providing educational services
- Demonstration of ample student success and satisfaction
- Truthful advertising
- Financial ability to deliver high-quality educational service

The NHSC publishes a directory of accredited home-study schools, which is available free of charge from:

The National Home Study Council
1601 18th Street NW
Washington, DC 20009
(202) 234-5100

THE ANNENBERG/CPB TELECOURSE

You can take a college course at home by turning on the television. The Annenberg/CPB project, in conjunction with the Corporation for Public Broadcasting, offers thirteen-week semester courses broadcast over public television, which can let students earn college credits. Accompanying materials, including texts and study guides, are available. Topics include issues such as saving the planet, the seasons of life, and learning in the computer age. The Annenberg/CPB project maintains a large audio-print course collection available for group or individual instruction extending from the humanities and social sciences to natural sciences and mathematics. This material can be used to satisfy your personal learning objectives or may be applied toward a college degree through enrollment in the University of Wisconsin Extension Program.

Annenberg/CPB Project
1111 16th Street NW
Washington, DC 20036
(800) LEARNER or (805) 968-2291

PUBLICATIONS

The Independent Study Catalog (Princeton: Peterson's, 1989). The National University's Continuing Education Association's guide to correspondence instruction lists ten thousand high school, college, and graduate courses offered by more than seventy colleges and universities. It includes subjects available, hours needed for each course of study, and the person to contact to discuss the home-study program. To order, contact:

Peterson's
PO Box 2123
Princeton, NJ 08543-2123
(800) EDU-DATA
    in NJ and outside the US, call
(609) 243-9111

Home Study Opportunities, by Laurie M. Carlson (Crozert, VA: Betterway, 1989), is an encyclopedic guide to going to school by mail, including advice on how to get the most out of home study while avoiding the pitfalls. It covers programs that prepare students for second careers, hobbies, volunteer service, college degrees, or that provide self-enrichment. Each listing includes detailed course descriptions, admissions requirements, program completion times, costs, and information on available financial aid. To order, contact:

Betterway Publications, Inc.
Box 219
Crozert, VA 22932
(804) 823-5661

DISCUSSION GROUPS

Meeting with others to discuss topics of interest is an enjoyable way to increase your knowledge and remain intellectually stimulated. Through a lively exchange of ideas, group members learn from each other, express their opinions, and share their life experience. Organized discussions can be found at libraries, museums, senior centers, Y's, and religious organizations. Several foundations provide materials and guidance for organizing your own discussion groups.

THE GREAT BOOK FOUNDATION

The Great Book Foundation is an independent, nonprofit educational corporation that provides reading materials and leader-training workshops for individuals and groups interested in discussing the great works of literature. They offer carefully prepared materials for five different discussion series on the work of such masters as Chekhov, Aristotle, Kant, Marx, Sophocles, and Shakespeare. Groups usually meet every other week for two hours. The only requirement for joining or starting a group is an interest in literature.

If you would like to start your own group, the Great Book Foundation will help. Their booklet, "How to Start a Great Book Discussion Group" outlines the steps to organizing a group. They also hold two-day training sessions around the country for those interested in becoming discussion leaders. If you would like to join an existing group, the foundation will provide a listing of Great Book Discussion Groups in your community.

The Great Books Foundation
40 East Huron Street
Chicago, IL 60611-2782
(800) 222-5870

NATIONAL ISSUES FORUMS

The town meeting is an important American institution dating from colonial New England. The National Issues Forums and Study Circles are based on the concept that a democratic society depends on an informed citizenry. Though the work of government may be carried on by politicians, it is the people who set its direction and purpose. Each individual is therefore responsible for keeping informed about the important issues of their day.

NIF Forums provides opportunities for individuals to address issues of national concern. Each year, three topics with prominent impact on society are selected for discussion; recent topics have included AIDS, health care for the aging, the environment, freedom of speech, and the public debt. After extensively researching the topics, NIF issues a thirty- to forty-page, clearly written, nonpartisan issue book that outlines three or four possible alternatives for action. This information becomes the basis for a full exchange of ideas among participants.

National Issues Forums
100 Commons Road
Dayton, OH 45459-2777
(800) 433-7834
(800) 433-4819 (in Ohio)

GREAT DECISIONS

More than a quarter of a million people participate in the Great Decisions program sponsored by the Foreign Policy Association, a nonpartisan organization devoted to educating the public about world affairs. Every year, the Foreign Policy Association publishes a briefing book providing concise, clear, objective information on eight of the most important foreign-policy issues facing the nation, such as arms agreements, US trade and global markets, Latin American debt, and Persian Gulf relations. This resource becomes the basis of discussion for groups that meet in people's homes, community centers, libraries, and civic and religious halls all over the country. After studying the material and exchanging ideas, participants may present their views to members of Congress through opinion ballets tabulated by the FPA.

If you wish to participate in a Great Decisions program, the FPA will provide you with a list of Great Decisions leaders in your community. If you wish to organize your own group, FPA will help you get started.

Foreign Policy Association
Department of College and Community Programs
729 Seventh Avenue
New York, NY 10019
(212) 764-4050

AARP AUDIO-VISUAL PROGRAM

The Constitution: That Delicate Balance

The Institute of Lifetime Learning offers a video course based on the award-winning series, "The Constitution: That Delicate Balance." This six-part program explores controversial human rights questions in relation to the constitution. For information on borrowing the series for group discussions, write:

The Constitution
D-12869
Program Scheduling Office
601 E Street NW
Washington, DC 20049

LEARNING VACATIONS

No more papers, no more books may be a child's idea of vacation, but many adults feel the opposite way. To them, combining learning and travel is the ideal way to refresh and rejuvenate, and they find that the opportunity to immerse themselves in an intense learning experience is exhilarating. Luckily, there are many such programs to choose from. Academic institutions, alumni associations, museums, and non-profit organizations offer a variety of short courses, both in the US and abroad.

Programs vary widely. Before signing up, make sure your aims and the aims of the group are in accord. Accommodations range from rustic to first class and fees vary from moderate to very expensive. Room, board, and transportation are sometimes included, though not always. Most programs have no specific academic requirements.

ELDERHOSTEL

Elderhostel was designed specifically to meet the educational needs of active retirees. Offering a smorgasbord of intellectual delights, it combines the joys of learning with the excitement of travel. Short-term academic programs are held on the campuses of educational institutions around the world. Students may walk through the fall foliage of southern Minnesota while studying forest-resource management, study prehistoric Indian pottery of the southwest on the campus of the University of Arizona, or explore the Battle of Gettysburg at Gettysburg National Military Park. Those wishing to travel outside the US can study the archaeology and folk art of Mexico, explore firsthand life in the Soviet Union, or investigate Chinese culture.

From its humble beginning in 1975 with 220 pioneer hostlers at five colleges in New Hampshire, Elderhostel has grown to accommodate more than 222,000 Elderhostelers in more than fifteen thousand colleges and universities in the US and more than forty countries. Yet it continues to reflect the original concept of its founding fathers: that education can open a pathway to fulfillment and satisfaction in the later years of one's life.

Despite his chronic ailments and gradual loss of vision, Louis Kousin, a seventy-nine-year-old retired fundraiser from Cranford, NJ, studies poetry at local Elderhostel sites. "Some of us did not have enough schooling growing up," said Mr. Kousin (*New York Times*, May 21, 1989). "Now we can take advantage of a delightful and meaningful combination of education and vacation with people of similar inspiration. And it's on a campus, just the way the young folks do it. That, too, is an opportunity many of us missed out on. I think it has kept me alive. If I didn't have this, I'd sit around and worry about my health. I take my assignments seriously and get a tremendous kick out of sharing the new experiences with my wife." Bertha and Lewis Woodman, aged seventy-five and seventy-nine of Newbury, Massachusetts, have attended twenty programs. "It gives us the opportunity to travel inexpensively all over the country, something we never could have done otherwise. But it's not a freebie or cheap vacation. It's set up so that you must keep your brains expanding."

Elderhostel is available to anyone sixty years or over. Participants may be accompanied by a spouse or companion not younger than fifty. Previous education is unnecessary. Most US programs last one week. Overseas programs generally run twenty-one days. Three classes are offered at each session. You may attend all three classes if you wish; however, attendance at only one class is required. There are no grades. Neither homework nor credit is given. Simple, comfortable accommodations are provided by the host facility, usually consisting of a college dormitory room with two twin beds. The bathroom is down the hall. Single rooms are sometimes available at an extra charge. Fees are low and include room and board, the cost of classes, and a variety of extracurricular activities. Overseas registration includes the cost of transportation. For those who cannot afford the cost of attending, Elderhostel offers a limited number of "Hostelships."

To learn more about Elderhostel, write:

Elderhostel
Suite 400
80 Boylston Street
Boston, MA 02116-4899
(617) 426-7788

CORNELL'S ADULT UNIVERSITY

Cornell's Adult University has been treating adult learners to a week of the best that college life can offer for more than twenty years. Ninety percent who attend plan to return. That's probably why Summer CAU in Ithaca is the largest, most diverse college vacation program of its type in the country. Every summer, people of all ages and interests enjoy this unusual experience. You may come alone or bring a friend. Bring your children or grandchildren. There are programs to keep everyone happy.

A week at CAU starts on Sunday with orientation and a welcome party, where you meet your counselors and fellow students. Classes, beginning on Monday, are taught by members of Cornell's faculty who are experts in their fields. Subjects range from opera to how to be a success in America. The afternoons are spent enjoying Cornell's athletic facilities, lectures, outdoor concerts, plays, museums, and hiking trails. Each evening features a barbecue or "mystery dinner." The week ends with a banquet, followed by a faculty roast and graduation party.

Cornell's Adult University
626 Thurston Avenue
Ithaca, NY 14850-2490
(607) 255-6260

TRAVEL WITH SCHOLARS

Every summer, the University of California at Berkeley offers exciting opportunities to participate in liberal arts courses utilizing the resources of Europe's most fascinating cities. You can study impressionist and post-impressionist art in the museums of Paris, delve into Medieval literature at Oxford University, discover the beauty of Venice, learn firsthand why the French Riviera was a mecca for such artists as Picasso, Matisse, and Renoir, unveil the mysteries of Japan's three-thousand-year-old culture in Kyoto, go behind the scenes of London's illustrious theaters, or trace the history of Scotland through its enchanting countryside.

Classes are taught in English by members of Berkeley's outstanding faculty or experts from the host university. Enrollment is open to adults interested in serious study who have completed at least two years of college. You have the option to earn college credits. All students are required to prepare for this experience by advance reading.

University of California
Berkeley Extension
2223 Fulton Street
Berkeley, CA 94720
(415) 642-8840

FOUNDATION FOR EUROPEAN LANGUAGE AND EDUCATIONAL CENTERS

What better way to learn a language than in the country it is spoken? At the Foundation for European Languages' twenty-two language centers in France, Spain, Italy, Germany, Japan, and Switzerland, you actually live the language you are learning. Classroom sessions are augmented by excursions and special events that give you the opportunity to test your skills. Most students live with a host family where no English is spoken, which lets you exercise your language skills on a practical, daily basis.

Programs run from two to twelve weeks. There are no prerequisites. Beginning to advanced level classes are available. Students receive an evaluation and certificate of completion at the end of each program.

Council Travel
Attn: Eurocentre Department
205 East 42nd Street
New York, NY 10017
(212) 661-1414

OUTWARD BOUND

Outward Bound is the oldest and largest adventure-based educational organization in the United States. Each year, more than twenty thousand Outward Bound students learn to move beyond their perceived limits and discover their inner strengths and capabilities through challenging wilderness experiences. With nature as the teacher, students develop a strong sense of self-respect, mutual support, and responsibility for the environment. Overcoming the obstacles inherent in the wilderness better prepares the students to meet the challenges of everyday life. They learn firsthand the power of perseverance, teamwork, leadership, and goal-setting. Through exploring the grandeur of nature, they discover the wonders of themselves.

There are more than six hundred courses to choose from, including sailing, backpacking, canoeing, sea kayaking, white-water rafting, mountain climbing, skiing, and dogsledding. Courses last from eight days to three months and are conducted for the most part in remote wilderness areas of the United States. Each group consists of eight to ten students, most of whom have had little or no previous wilderness experience, and at least two instructors skilled in wilderness adventure and trained in the latest instructional and safety-management practices. Though it is not necessary to be an experienced outdoorsman or athlete to participate, Outward Bound is a challenging and demanding experience. Students carry their own food and gear with them and camp out at night. There are days of hiking and climbing and you can expect to loose a few pounds and experience some sore muscles as well as make new friends and have a lot of fun. Costs are minimal and include all equipment, food, and instruction. Students supply their own clothing, boots, and transportation to and from the site. For those unable to meet the costs, financial assistance is available.

Each Outward Bound course begins with a training phase in which students learn the basics of first aid, campcraft, orienteering, and their course activity. During the expedition phase, students build upon this knowledge and take on more responsibilities until they are ready for the solo phase, when they will be alone except for daily safety checks made by the staff. After this time of introspection and reflection, the group undertakes an endurance activity, which tests their capacity and leaves them feeling they can conquer anything. A final expedition without direct supervision by the staff concludes the trip.

Outward Bound offers many different kinds of courses, including a special course for adults over fifty-five called Going Beyond. In this course, participants stretch beyond their perceived limits and learn that age and physical ability are no barrier to discovering their unknown talents, abilities, and true capabilities. Joe Alexander, a sixty-three-year-old retired industrial-relations manager, met the challenge and learned he could do things he never thought he was capable of before. He was hesitant at first to join Outward Bound because he didn't know if he was physically able to complete the trip. But while he found the course demanding, he was never faced with anything he could not conquer. "We learned to rely on each other," he said. Though he was always afraid of heights, he successfully completed a rope-climbing course, which left him feeling elated. After nine days in the wilderness, he no longer questions his abilities and is preparing for a second Outward Bound course this winter to climb volcanoes in Mexico.

Outward Bound USA
384 Field Point Road
Greenwich, CT 06830
(800) 243-8520

PUBLICATIONS

Learning Vacations, by Gerson G. Eisenberg (Princeton: Peterson's, 1989), a guidebook to over four hundred learning vacation opportunities, can be obtained through Peterson's guides. It provides full details on each program, including content, duration, accommodations, costs, and whom to contact. Opportunities range from art and archaeology to Zen and Zoology. For ordering information, call toll free:

Peterson's
PO Box 2123
Princeton, NJ 08543-2123
(800) EDU-DATA
in NJ and outside the US, call
 (609) 243-9111

The Guide to Academic Travel, by Lawrence Caplan and Darlene Shane (Coral Gables, FL: Shaw Guides, 1990), contains detailed descriptions of programs offered by 258 colleges, museums, historical societies, nature and environmental organizations, travel companies, and individuals. Topics include anthropology, art history, botany, world affairs, environmental issues, literature, music, philosophy, religion, sociology, and more. Each listing contains details on dates, academic content, faculty, costs, and contact information. The guide to academic travel is available in bookstores or may be purchased through Shaw Guides:

Shaw Guides, Inc.
625 Biltmore Way
Coral Gables, FL 33134
(305) 446-8888

CHAPTER IV

Avocations

We don't stop playing because we get old.
We get old because we stop playing.

ANONYMOUS

An avocation is an occupation pursued for personal rather than financial rewards. That does not mean it isn't taken seriously. A true avocation is completely absorbing and demands your best. The term "hobby" has come to mean a pastime. Amateur is synonymous with unskilled. Yet doing something purely for the love of it can result in the highest level of accomplishment. Professionals are people who support themselves with their efforts, but payment is not necessarily a measure of ability or competence. If it were, Van Gogh would not be considered a true artist, since he was never able to derive his livelihood from his painting. In fact, working for pay may actually be a detriment. Professional artists and athletes often confess they did their best work before they turned "pro."

What interests you purely for its own sake often reveals where your talent lies. Perhaps talent is actually an intense

115

focusing of energy. If you examine talented people, you will find incredible dedication, determination, discipline, and willingness to sacrifice for what they love. When you watch a skater do a perfect triple jump, you do not see the years of practice, sweat, and pain it took to execute that one exquisite movement.

You may already be what you always wanted, save for semantics. For instance, your less-than-perfect body, shyness, and financial obligations have kept you from a dance career. Yet you maintain the same passion for dance you did as a child when you cried because the ballet was over. You are a patron of your local ballet company and have season tickets. You are educated in the history of dance and read biographies of famous dancers. You sent two little girls to dance class and lived through their recitals. You love a social occasion that includes dancing and do a mean waltz. If someone would call you a dancer you would disagree. But redefine dancer and you will see that you are.

You do not need to justify to anyone why you like something. If it has validity for you, go for it. Houdini must have looked pretty silly tying himself up with rope before his genius was recognized. We are somehow drawn toward what we are best suited for. When we concentrate on what brings us joy we discover the best of ourselves.

COLLECTING

We are all born collectors. As children, we comb beaches searching for stones and shells, pile marbles into jars, hoard comic books, and trade baseball cards. Our interest in accumulating, displaying, and searching out the items that fascinate us may get more sophisticated as we grow older, but it does not go away. People collect everything: antiques, banks, beer cans, bottles, buttons, cars, Disney characters, inkwells, matchbooks, movie memorabilia, postcards, salt-and-pepper shakers, sheet music, and valentines. The list is endless. There probably is no item you can think of that someone doesn't collect. If there is something that has caught your imagination and sent you rummaging through flea markets, attics, and secondhand stores in search of your treasure, you can be certain others share your passion. There are clubs, conventions, exhibits, and publications for almost any collectible item.

Collecting can open up a world of adventure for the enthusiast. The secret is finding an area of interest that appeals to you in a personal way. Perhaps you have some nostalgic connection with an object from childhood or from your occupation. Your enjoyment can take you beyond the thrill of seeking and finding to researching the history and background of the objects, the methods used to make them, and the political and social background that makes the items you collect special. You can have the pleasure of showing off your treasures and socializing with others who share your interest.

One collector with a passion for Marilyn Monroe memorabilia reads every book she can find on the subject, studies all Marilyn's movies, and collects photos. Since Marilyn is the most photographed and mass-marketed woman in the world, a collection of her images could fill a museum, but like most collectors this one has specialized. Her greatest thrill is discovering early stills from Norma Jean's commercial modeling career, which are sometimes found in magazines of the period by an astute eye. Friends help her increase her collection. She has an uncanny knack for ferreting out treasures in unlikely places. For instance, she discovered an original print of Marilyn's famous calendar in a second-hand store while on vacation in Rhode Island. To the uninitiated, it may seem that the subject of Marilyn Monroe has been played out, but to the enthusiast there are always challenges. Every once in a while, new shots are discovered, diaries found, old footage recovered. There are always questions to ponder. For instance, where is the footage of her first screen appearance, which Twentieth-Century Fox cut out of *Scudda Hoo! Scudda Hay?* Such questions fascinate collectors.

To get started in collecting, all you need to do is select a category that interests you and start investigating. Learn all you can. The public library is always a good place to start. Collectors magazines are excellent references. They have information about events, organizations, and suppliers. Get to know others who share your interest. Collectors clubs exist for most things you can think of. Clubs provide opportunities to trade, share information, and socialize with people of similar interest. Most organizations publish newsletters, hold meetings, conventions, and seminars. To locate an organization dedicated to your interest, check the *Encyclopedia of Associations* at your public library. Also, the *Standard Directory of Periodicals* is a good source for locating publications.

Searching out the items you wish to collect can be a real adventure. Keep your eyes open for flea markets, tag sales, and auctions. All are good sources for building your collection. If you buy at auctions, make sure you know what you are doing. Never bid on anything you have not inspected prior to the auction. Decide on your top price and stick to it. It is easy to get carried away by the excitement and end up spending more than you should. Other good sources for collectibles are advertisements in publications, shows, fellow collectors, and dealers. When you find a dealer you like and trust, you can give him or her a list of what you are looking for and ask to be called when an item appears.

Collecting need not be an expensive hobby. Many collectible items can be purchased for less than ten dollars. On the other hand, some rare items command huge sums. Collecting can be more than just an enjoyable hobby. Some people collect for investment. But, like the stock market, collecting can be risky business, especially for the novice. Before making any major purchases, be sure you know what you are doing. Check with several experts and be careful. There are many scams and false claims about collectibles. Be especially leery of new-issue collectibles, such as first-edition plates, spoons, thimbles, and coins with large advertising and promotion campaigns. Lifetime investment opportunities rarely come in the mail or are advertised on TV.

BOOKS AND OTHER PUBLICATIONS

Collectibles, by Mariam Klamkin (Garden City, NY: Doubleday, 1981) is an excellent reference book. She provides information on more than eighty categories of collectibles, including books, clubs, dealers, and repairs.

The following dealers specialize in collectors books. Write to them for free lists of available books:

Collector Books Clearing
 House
PO Box 3009
Paducah, KY 42002-3009
(502) 898-6211

Edmonds Books
PO Box 143, Highway 60
Ledbetter, KY 42058-0143

The Reference Rack
Box 44C
Orefield, PA 18069
(800) 722-7279

Chilton Book Company
One Chilton Way
Radnor, PA 19089
(800) 345-1214

Some general periodicals available to collectors include:

Antiques and Collecting, a monthly magazine, features articles on many types of collectibles, including glass and china, political memorabilia, furniture, jewelry, etc. It also contains market reports, auction news, show calendars, and book reviews.

Antiques and Collecting
1006 South Michigan Avenue
Chicago, IL 60605
(312) 939-4767

Collector Editions is published monthly by Collector Communications. It features articles on a variety of topics of interest to collectors, including information on products and services, an "ask the expert section," an auction report, and book reviews. Other magazines published by Collector Communications include *Dolls, Dollmaking, Teddy Bear Review,* and *Miniature Collector.*

Collector Communications
170 Fifth Avenue
New York, NY 10010
(212) 645-8976

American Collectors Journal is a monthly newsletter with up-to-date information on events in the world of collecting. Feature articles highlight many different kinds of collectibles. A classified advertising section is included as well as a calendar of events.

American Collectors Journal
PO Box 407
Kewanee, IL 61443
(309) 853-8441

STAMP COLLECTING

Stamp collecting is reputed to be the most popular hobby in the world. It is estimated that there are 19 million philatelists (people who collect and study postage stamps) in the United

States alone. What is it about stamps that fascinates so many people? It is as if they hold some magical quality that sends the imagination soaring to other worlds and times. Through these tiny windows, you travel through space, visit famous people, witness great events, learn about birds, banking, boating, or baseball. Whatever subject excites your interest can come alive through stamps.

Who has not at one time been caught by the beauty of these little pictures and wondered about them? Perhaps you had a collection when you were a child. Why not dust it off and start again? If you never had a collection, getting started is easy. Everyone with a mailbox has access to stamps. Family and friends can help by saving envelopes for you. The post office provides a readily accessible source. The classified ads in philatelic newspapers and magazines are another important source for the collector. Variety and hobby stores also sell packets of stamps. Almost every city has stamp clubs where you can meet fellow philatelists who will be glad to pass along information and share duplicates.

The key to enjoying your collection is to save stamps that really excite your interest. Do you love animals? baseball? dinosaurs? Was there a time in history you would like to have lived in? What places would you like to visit? Who would you like to have met? There are many different ways to organize a collection. Some people start by collecting as many stamps from as many different countries as they can. Others select one particular country. Another way to organize a collection is by theme, such as sports, horses, space, transportation, art, or a particular date, such as your birthday. Some people save only mint or used stamps. Others collect multiples in blocks or strips. Errors, freaks, and oddities are a popular specialty, as are envelopes or cards used as mail communication, called covers.

Jerome W. Howe, a retired technical-journal editor, has

been an avid stamp collector for many years. After his retirement, he decided to combine his interest in stamps with a boyhood interest in ships. He considered collecting stamps with lighthouses, steamships, and sail boats, then settled on covers with maritime-related postal markings that had crossed the high seas on actual sailing ships and steamers. He traced one nineteenth-century manuscript and cover through a postal history that began in Paris on September 9, 1855, then to London, Liverpool, America via Cunard steamer, finally ending in Boston.

The US Postal Service maintains a division that sells mint stamps (commemorative and regular-issue mint stamps) as well as guidebooks, stamp collecting kits, and exhibition cards. Purchases may be made in person at many post offices nationwide or by mail from:

US Postal Service
Philatelic Sales Division
Washington, DC 20265

To keep up-to-date on available US stamps, send a postcard or letter to the above address and ask to be placed on the Philatelic Catalog mailing list. Every other month you will receive a full-color, illustrated price list of all current US stamps.

To locate a stamp club in your area, contact:

Linn's Club Center
PO Box 29
Sidney, OH 45365-0029
(513) 498-2111

American Philatelic Society

The American Philatelic Society, organized in 1866, is the oldest and largest organization of stamp collectors. Its membership exceeds 50,000 and includes people in more than one hundred countries. It offers many services to its members, including by-mail use of the largest public-access philatelic library in the country, collection insurance, an intermember buying and selling service, and a subscription to *The American Philatelist*, an outstanding monthly journal. There are 700 local chapters of the American Philatelic Society, whose members meet regularly to exchange information and share their interest. Over one hundred regional shows, where members exhibit collections, are held around the country each year. A national convention is held annually.

The American Philatelic Society will send a free beginners information packet upon request. For this packet or membership information, send a legal-size self-addressed stamped envelope to:

Education Department–R
American Philatelic Society
PO Box 8000
State College, PA 16803
(814) 237-3803

Courses

The American Philatelic Society in conjunction with Pennsylvania State University offers both home-study and summer-seminar courses for the stamp collector. The summer sessions are one week long and cover such topics as fakes and forgeries, buying and selling, and specialty collecting. The instructors include well-known experts in specialized areas of collecting and leaders in the commercial side of the hobby. Home-study courses for beginning, intermediate, and advanced students are conducted under the guidance of renowned specialists. Students may establish a dialogue through the mail with the course author and instructor.

For information on seminars contact:

Education Department–R
American Philatelic Society
PO Box 8000
State College, PA 16803

For information on home-study courses, contact:

Department of Independent Learning
128 Mitchell Building
Pennsylvania State University
University Park, PA 16802
(800) 458-3617

Publications

The following weekly newspapers keep stamp enthusiasts informed on prices, market values, new issues, recently disclosed errors or forgeries, shows, auctions, and dealers; they also run feature articles.

Linn's Stamp News
PO Box 29
Sidney, OH 45365-0029
(513) 498-2111

Stamp Collector
PO Box 10
Albany, OR 97321
(503) 928-3569

Stamps
85 Cantisteo Street
Hornell, NY 14843
(607) 324-2212

COIN COLLECTING

Numismatics, the study of coins, medals, tokens, and paper money is one of the oldest hobbies in the world. People have been fascinated by coins since they were first introduced in the mid-seventh century BC. Coins are not only a representation of wealth but are miniature works of art, pieces of history, and clues to other civilizations. Because people have always accumulated and saved coins, surviving specimens represent numismatic history. Today there are 3 million Americans who share an interest in coin collecting.

Starting a coin collection is easy. You probably have a few coins tucked away that came down to you from your grandfather, that you picked up in your travels, or that you just like to keep around for some reason. Look at the change in your pocket. You've already started a collection. The next thing you need is a good basic reference book. *A Guide Book to United States Coins*, by R. S. Yeoman (Racine, WI: Western, 1991) commonly referred to as "The Red Book," is the bible of collectors. Ask for it in the library or get a copy at your local bookstore. Hobby shops and variety stores are good sources for supplies. Publications are available on newsstands. The American Numismatic Association publishes a monthly magazine and newspapers run regular columns. There are coin clubs in most communities where you can enjoy the friendship of other numismatists and share information. Conventions and shows give you the opportunity to increase your knowledge of your hobby, make new acquisitions, and exhibit your collection.

Because the value of a coin increases if it is in good condition, you'll want to take care of those you collect. Don't store them where they can get dented or scratched. Store them in pressed-board albums, coin folders, or paper coin envelopes. Loose dirt may be carefully removed with soap and water but never attempt any further cleaning yourself. This should be done only by an expert. A coin preserved by nature that maintains the coloration of age is more desirable than one that has been cleaned or polished.

Coin collecting need not be an expensive hobby. There are thousands of coins available for under a dollar. But if you are considering coins as an investment, be very careful. The Federal Trade Commission and the American Numismatic Association have issued a warning on rare-coin scams to potential investors. They urge you to contact them for their free consumer-alert brochure before making any major investment.

American Numismatic Association

The American Numismatic Association was organized in 1891 and has a current membership of 31,000 members. It is the only hobby-related organization chartered by Congress. ANA members enjoy a free monthly magazine, *The Numismatist*, filled with news and events. They also have direct access to the ANA's decade-old grading service, use of the world's largest circulating library of numismatic material, and the opportunity to join with thousands of collectors at the exciting conventions held twice a year in various cities where you can participate in educational seminars, bid for rare and valuable coins, and view outstanding collections. The ANA also offers discounts on insurance, travel, and coin-grading seminars.

For a free booklet, "Coin Collecting," tips on investing in rare coins, or membership information, send a self-addressed, stamped, legal-size envelope to:

American Numismatic Association
818 North Cascade Avenue
Colorado Springs, CO 80903-3279
(719) 632-2646

Coin World

Coin World is a weekly newspaper keeping numismatists up to date on the latest trends and issues in the world of coins. Feature articles deal with such topics as regulation of coin dealers and profiles of collectors. Regular departments include information on shows, auctions, and clubs. A classified-advertising section lists opportunities for buyers and sellers of all kinds of coin-related collectibles.

The editors of *Coin World* newspaper also publish a comprehensive guidebook to the world of coins, *Coin World Almanac*, which is now in its sixth edition. It includes a summary of newsmaking numismatic events from 1987 through 1990, record auction prices, and minting listings as well as advice on rare coins and investments and up-to-date market information.

Coin World's annual *Guide to Coin Valuations and Trends*, published for every series of United States coins, presents an easy-to-use resource for the collector. It includes an explanation of confusing grading terms and an analysis of the coin market. Mints, mint marks, and rarities are included as well as information on how to collect.

The *Coin World* staff has also put together a beginners guide to collecting coins and paper money. It will teach you all you need to know to get started. You will learn how and where to buy and sell, what grading is and why it is important, how paper money and coins are made, and how to meet other collectors.

Coin World
PO Box 150
Sidney, OH 45365-0029
(513) 498-0800

Other Publications

Numismatic News is a weekly coin-collecting newspaper featuring Coin Market, a price guide to popular US coins. It is designed for the active collector and investor and includes an auction calendar, show directory, and advertising index as well as editorial features.

Numismatic News
Circulation Department
700 East State Street
Iola, WI 54990-0001
(715) 445-2214

DOLL COLLECTING

Doll collecting is reputed to be the second largest hobby in the United States. Why do so many people love dolls? Perhaps they bring out the child in us, make us think of our own childhood, or remind us of when our children were young. Maybe they fill an empty nest or fulfill a need to nurture and protect. Dolls can represent mankind in miniature, the dress and customs of various times and places. Whatever the reason, the serious collecting of dolls is far from child's play. Doll collectors need to be extremely knowledgeable about their hobby. They must know the history, design, costuming, construction, reconstruction, rarity, and value of dolls. This knowledge comes from painstaking research. You must study books and magazines, visit museum collections, and communicate with other collectors.

The first step in starting any collection is studying all you can. Read all you can find, subscribe to publications, visit collections and shows, and get to know other collectors through clubs or conventions. Then select an area for specialization. Dolls come in all forms and sizes, from miniatures to life-size. They are made of cloth, felt, china, wood, wax, plastic, rubber, and bisque, perhaps the most rare and beautiful of all materials. You may wish to collect dolls of a certain era, country, material, ethnic group, film character, or the work of a specific artist. Or perhaps you wish to specialize in baby dolls, boy dolls, or teenage dolls. You can start your collection with the dolls you or your family and friends saved or go in search of a favorite doll you had or wanted to have as a child. Dolls can be found in attics, flea markets, garage sales, auctions, shows, shops, through ads in hobby magazines, or through other collectors. When making your selection, pay special attention to the distinctiveness of the head. This is the most important price-setting feature. Also look for originality, appropriateness, and authenticity of the costume. You will want to collect dolls that are in the best possible condition and have been restored and dressed to appear as much as possible as they did when new.

Your interest in doll collecting can lead to an involvement in repairing and restoring dolls, making dolls, or exhibiting your collection in private doll museums. Marietta Wilcox and Winifred Johnson, both graduates of the Lifetime Career School's Doll Hospital School, are well known for their extensive collections. Marietta, who has eight grandchildren, operates Marietta's House of Dolls in Bergen, New York. Her collection consists of a United Nations of foreign dolls and a "White House Blue Room" filled with dignitaries. Winifred began collecting dolls when her son left home for the service in 1942. Dolls began arriving from Germany, Korea, and Japan as he traveled throughout the world. Even after he returned home, her collection continued to grow. Today their collection includes 250 dolls from all over the world. Winifred operates the "Mi-Doll Hospital" in Exeter, New Hampshire, named after the first doll she had as a child.

Seventy-one-year old Earline Rytel of Columbus, Ohio, ran an antique clothing shop on the campus of Ohio State University before her retirement. She became interested in dolls when a friend asked her to help dress a doll. She is now president of a doll club that meets once a month to hear speakers on topics of interest and to share information. The club holds an annual doll sale to raise funds for children's charities. Earline is not content to just collect dolls: she learns all about them. She studies the dress, customs, and history of the period for each doll she owns. To Earline, dolls are not just toys but works of art.

United Federation of Dolls Clubs

The United Federation of Dolls Clubs was founded in 1949 to preserve, display, and disseminate information about doll collecting. They hold regular meetings and conventions and publish a newsletter, *Doll News*. They will help you locate a doll club in your area.

United Federation of Dolls Clubs, Inc.
8-B East Street
PO Box 14152
Parkville, MO 64152
(816) 741-1002

The Doll Hospital School

Lifetime Career Schools offers a home-study training program covering doll collecting, repair, making, designing, and doll clothing as well as instruction on how to own and operate your own doll hospital. The course includes fully illustrated lesson material, supply kits, patterns, and a twelve-month subscription to *Doll Doings*, a newsletter featuring articles of special interest to doll enthusiasts. The course is fully accredited by the National Home Study Council.

The Doll Hospital School
Lifetime Career Schools
2251 Barry Avenue
Los Angeles, CA 90064
(213) 478-0617

Books and Other Publications

Hobby House Press has a large selection of books on all topics related to doll collecting, including antique and modern collecting, dressing, and price guides. They also offer books on doll making, paper dolls, miniatures, fashion history, and Teddy Bears. For a free catalogue of available books, write to:

Hobby House Press, Inc.
900 Fredrick Street
Cumberland, MD 21502
(301) 759-4940

Hobby magazines are excellent sources for information on such topics as collectible and modern dolls, artist's dolls, and the making and costuming of dolls. They also feature a geographical listing of doll shows and events and classified sections on dolls and supplies.

Doll Reader
Hobby House Press, Inc.
900 Fredrick Street
Cumberland, MD 21502
(301) 759-4940

Dolls
Collector Communication, Inc.
170 Fifth Avenue
New York, NY 10010
(212) 989-8700

Dollmaking
Collector Communication, Inc.
170 Fifth Avenue
New York, NY 10010
(212) 989-8700

For information on doll repair, check your phone book. A catalogue of doll supplies, including parts, wigs, reproduction china and bisque parts, shoes, eyes, eyelashes, and stands can be obtained through:

Standard Doll Company
23-83 31st Street
Long Island City, NY 11105
(718) 721-7787

GAMES

There is more to games than fun. They challenge you, bring you together with other people, and exercise your mind. A recent study conducted at Scripps College in Claremont, California, suggests that playing bridge enhances memory and reasoning. According to the authors of the study, Louise Clarkson-Smith and Alan A. Hartley, such "exercise may help forestall degenerative changes in the brain associated with normal aging. So play bridge, do crossword puzzles, or take up computers: all of these activities may slow the rate of normal decline. But if you want to keep a really sharp mind, don't ignore physical exercise." As they say, use it or lose it.

CHESS

Whether you're a novice or a pro, the US Chess Federation can help you become involved in the challenge and excitement of chess. With more than 60,000 members ranging in age from four to one hundred and four, and with more than 1,000 affiliated clubs around the country, you'll never lack a partner. They'll team you up with players of your ability level at a club near you and provide opportunities for tournament competition and chess by mail. They'll offer you discounts on products and equipment from all over the world. You'll receive a subscription to their monthly magazine, "Chess Life," filled with chess lessons, game analyses, tips from leading masters, great games played by grand masters, and articles on such things as chess-playing computers. If you've never played the game, they will send you free instructions and tips on how to win.

US Chess Federation
186 Route 9W
New Windsor, NY 12553
(800) 388-KING

BRIDGE

Bridge is the most popular game in the world. More than 12 million people play bridge in America alone. It is a favorite activity of older adults. According to the American Contract Bridge League, the average age of their nearly 200,000 members is fifty-seven. Bridge is fun, inexpensive, and challenging. It involves risk, evaluation, judgment, and logic. Bridge is a great way to socialize and can be enjoyed by anyone regardless of their skill level.

The American Contract Bridge League invites you to join one of its 4,200 clubs for friendly games and tournament play. Members receive the *Bulletin*, a monthly magazine with information on upcoming tournaments and tips from the experts. Members are also entitled to discounts on playing cards, books, and other supplies. If you join ACBL, you can find a game anywhere in the country. The annual *Directory of Clubs* will let you know where to find other players.

American Contract Bridge League
2990 Airways Boulevard
Memphis, TN 38116-3847
(800) 444-ACBL

PUZZLES

Puzzle buffs can join with thousands of others who love testing their word skills through Puzzle Buffs International. Members receive a history of puzzles, discounts on puzzles books, and a quarterly newsletter filled with games, puzzles, and news.

Puzzle Buffs International
1772 State Road
Cuyahoga Falls, OH 44223
(216) 923-2397

ADAPTIVE GAMES

If you have difficulty with diminishing manual dexterity or loss of vision, you can still continue to play your favorite games. Several companies specialize in adapting games to your needs. Larger pieces, large print, braille, and textured and brightly colored elements aid in identifying and grasping game pieces. Cards, jigsaw puzzles, dominoes, Chinese checkers, chess, checkers, backgammon, bingo, poker chips, Monopoly, and many more games are available in adaptive versions. Catalogues are available from the following sources:

Consumer Products
American Foundation for the Blind
15 West 16th Street
New York, NY 10011
(212) 620-2000

World Wide Games
Colchester, CT 06415

Flaghouse
150 North MacQuesten Parkway
Mount Vernon, NY 10550
(800) 699-1900

GENEALOGY

Was your great-grandfather really a cattle baron in the old country, or was that before they hung him? Discover the truth about your family history. Genealogy, tracing your family roots, takes you on a fascinating journey through your own lineage and will unearth a living, breathing history complete with the joys and pathos of human experience. You will not just document names and dates, but learn of fortunes made and lost, love and lust, wars and famines, heroes and rogues. In the process, you will meet and correspond with long-lost relatives, find inspiration for vacation trips, amass a scrapbook of letters, photos, and documents, and construct a family chart. The fruits of your efforts will produce an heirloom to be cherished by generations to come.

Like solving a detective mystery, tracing your roots requires painstaking research and presents many challenges. You may discover a source that takes you back many generations, or you may suddenly hit a dead end that requires creativity and ingenuity to overcome. Fortunately, many avenues of research are available to you. No matter what your family background is, there are organizations and societies to aid you in your search. It doesn't matter if your family came over on the Mayflower, a slave vessel, or commercial steamer, or if you are of Polish, German, Jewish, African, Irish, Native American, or any other descent. Even if you are an orphan and have no idea where your ancestors came from, there is an organization that can help you. There are books, maps, libraries, and archives available to genealogists as well as computer programs and publications.

Start with what you know. Write down everything you know about your family. What was your father's name and his date and place of birth. What was your grandmother's maiden name? Did she have brothers and sisters? Contact family members and ask what names, dates, and stories they recall. Collect all the records you can find, such as marriage and death certificates, deeds, wills, diplomas, obituaries, and family photos (be sure to look at what's written on the back). The family bible may prove an invaluable source. Visit graves and note the inscriptions on the gravestones. Write to the church or synagogue family members attended.

When you have pieced together all you can find, you may

turn to government sources for available records. Many are housed in local courthouses. A US census has been taken every ten years since 1790. Immigrants were required to give the year of their arrival and date and place of birth. Records up to 1910 are available to researchers and can reveal additional names and relationships. To trace ancestors born in another country, you can investigate naturalization records and ships' passenger lists.

There are many excellent genealogical libraries throughout the country. To locate one in your area, consult *The Directory of Historical Societies and Agencies in the US and Canada* (Nashville, TN: the American Association for State and Local History, 1990), or *The Directory of American Libraries with Genealogical or Local History Collections*, by P. William Filby (Wilmington, DE: Scholarly Resources, 1988). The three largest collections of genealogical information are the Genealogical Society of the Church of Jesus Christ of Latter-Day Saints (popularly known as the Mormons) in Salt Lake City, the New York Public Library, and the Library of Congress in Washington, DC.

Because the Mormons believe in the eternal nature of family ties, which obligates them to search out their ancestors, the Family History Library maintained by the Mormons in Salt Lake City and its 1,500 branch centers houses the largest collection of genealogical records in the world. You may write for a complete list of services to:

Family History Library
The Church of Jesus Christ of Latter-Day Saints
35 Northwest Temple Street
Salt Lake City, UT 84150
(801) 240-2331

The New York Public Library maintains an enormous collection of printed materials related to genealogy, including books, pamphlets, maps, letters, diaries, portraits, state and local histories, and military records. If you are unable to visit the library in person, you may request a photocopy of the information you require from the photocopy service division. Be sure to ask for an estimate of services first. This kind of research can get very expensive.

The New York Public Library
Genealogy Division, Room 315N-M
Fifth Avenue and 42nd Street
New York, NY 10018
(212) 340-0833

The Library of Congress has the largest collection of printed books on genealogy. It maintains town histories, local histories, and family histories. It is not necessary to visit the library itself to access this information. Local public libraries are linked by computer to most information available.

US Library of Congress
Washington, DC 20540
(202) 707-5537

The National Archives in Washington, DC, and its regional branches maintain millions of records relating to people who have had dealings with the federal government. The most useful to genealogists include census, military, pension, passenger-ship arrival, naturalization, and land records. The National Archives publishes several information booklets that will help you in your research, including:

"Aids for Genealogical Research"
"Using Records in the National Archives for Genealogical Research"

"Using Census Records"
"Military Service Records in the National Archives"
"Guide to Records in the National Archives"

National Archives Records Service
General Service Administration
Washington, DC 20408
(202) 501-5402

Employing a Professional

At some point you may wish to employ the services of a professional genealogist who specializes in a particular geographical area, ethnic group, time period, or type of record. It is advisable to contact several professionals before deciding who will be right for you. Always ask for their credentials: their professional affiliations, educational background, and publication record. What foreign languages do they speak? What records do they have access to? Are they skilled in the specific area of your search? Be sure to discuss fees. Do they charge by the hour? Will you be billed for out-of-pocket expenses? Be careful of unrestricted research. Authorizing research to be billed to you later may prove to be more expensive than you thought. You may wish to prepay expenses and thereby limit the research to be done. It is up to you to define for your researcher what you want. Do you wish to trace one family line or all? Your researcher should provide you with an initial survey of published sources readily available and an estimate of possible research success. Be sure to reach an agreement before any work begins.

The following organizations can also help you locate a professional:

Association of Professional Genealogists
PO Box 11601
Salt Lake City, UT 84147-1601

For a roster, send a self-addressed, stamped envelope and identification of geographic or topical specialization needed.

Board of Certification of Genealogists
PO Box 19165
Washington, DC 20036-0165

Accredited Genealogists
Family History Library
35 North West Temple Street
Salt Lake City, UT 84150

For a roster, send a self-addressed, stamped envelope and identification of geographic or topical specialization needed.

NATIONAL GENEALOGICAL SOCIETY

Membership in the National Genealogical Society entitles family researchers to a wide range of services. Access to the society's research library containing family histories, local histories, reference books, periodicals, and manuscripts is available by mail. Members receive the *National Genealogical Society Quarterly* containing scholarly papers, source material, and book reviews and the bimonthly NGS newsletter featuring reports on the genealogical community, potential sources, library acquisitions, and members queries. Discounts are available for publications and educational services; an annual conference brings together professionals and hobbyists alike for lectures and exchange of information.

The National Genealogical Society offers a home-study course in the basics of American genealogy. The course covers such topics as how to find the records you need, how to search systematically, how to document each item, how to evaluate genealogical evidence, and how to maintain orderly family records. For information about the course, contact the NGS's education department.

National Genealogical Society
4527 17th Street North
Arlington, VA 22207-2399
(703) 525-0050

GENEALOGICAL COMPUTING

Home computers can be a valuable tool for genealogists. They allow you to store, sort, retrieve, and access vast amounts of information. With the help of computer technology, you can print family trees or publish a family history as well as search data bases and communicate with other genealogists. *Genealogical Computing*, a quarterly journal published by Ancestry, is an excellent source for computer genealogy information. Articles include the pros and cons of genealogy software, reviews of new products, and a special beginners section. Genealogical computing maintains directories of computer-interest groups, data bases, software, and electronic bulletin boards.

Ancestry Publishing
Genealogical Computing
PO Box 476
Salt Lake City, UT 84110
(801) 531-1790

Genealogical Software

Family Tree Maker is a software program that provides a simple, quick method for creating family trees. You enter the names, dates, birthplaces, and any other information you wish to include on a fill-in-the-data form, and Family Tree Maker builds a data base that automatically draws family trees complete with boxes for each individual and lines to show relationships. You can show the pedigree of one individual or trace your entire family roots back ninety-nine generations. You can even construct photo trees of three generations. The instruction manual includes tips and sources to help you in your research.

Family Tree Maker
Banner Blue Software, Inc.
PO Box 7865
Fremont, CA 94537

Family Roots is a comprehensive genealogy research program designed as a working tool for the beginning and advanced genealogist. It is capable of serving many functions. It can store basic family information using defined fields and can automatically store information common to several people. It can produce four types of ancestor charts and two descendant charts. It has the ability to view all information on one person in a single page format or trace an ancestral line on the screen by stepping from child to parent. The program also has a method of storing histories, anecdotes, and notes. Family Roots is simple to use and comes with an easy-to-follow manual, and toll-free phone and mail support.

Family Roots
Quinsept, Inc.
PO Box 216
Lexington, MA 02173
(800) 637-7668

BOOKS, PUBLICATIONS, AND SUPPLIES

Sales Department
National Genealogical Society
4527 17th Street North
Arlington, VA 22207-2399
(703) 525-0050
Sells guides, records, books, and supplies. A list is available upon request.

Genealogy Publishing Co., Inc.
1001 North Calvert Street
Baltimore, MD 21202
(301) 837-8271
Free catalogue of books, general reference aids, local history, and immigration records is available.

Genealogy Unlimited, Inc.
Department F
PO Box 537
Orem, UT 84059-0537
(800) 666-4363
A free catalogue of books, supplies, and maps is available.

Goodspeed's Book Shop, Inc.
7 Beacon Street
Boston, MA 02108
(617) 523-5970
Free catalogue of books, guides, and family histories is available.

Ancestry
PO Box 476
Salt Lake City, UT 84110-0476
(800) 531-1790
Free catalogue of books and guides is available; Ancestry also sponsors a research club.

PERSONAL COMPUTERS

People have always been fascinated by their machines but no machine has been more beguiling than the computer. From the first stroke of the keyboard, a bonding begins. As information is received and exchanged, the relationship deepens. Before you know it, the hum of the disc drive is music to your ears and you are contemplating all the things you can do together. You no longer remember how you ever got along without one.

Computers may be man's most important invention since the wheel. Yet many of the most experienced members of society are among the last to grasp this powerful tool. Children are introduced to computers at school. Working adults learn to operate them on the job. But many older adults havׅ not been exposed to computer technology, yet they have much to gain from and to contribute to the computer age.

If you are not computer literate, this is a good time to learn. Today's personal computers (PCs) are very friendly. You can take them home, plug them in, click a few keys to bring up your training program, and start right in. You don't have to know a lot of technical terms to purchase one. You don't even have to shop in a computer store. Many department stores and mass-merchandise chains have computer departments. Recognizing the potential of the older market, companies are starting to pay attention to the special needs of this group, such as by providing magnified screens and large-print manuals and word-processing programs. Seventy-two-year-old E. B. Clark of Seattle decided it was time he became computer literate when he watched a seven-year-old boy operate a PC. "How'd you learn to work it?" he asked. "What are you, some kind of dummy?" the kid replied (*Time*, February 12, 1990).

You can use computers to balance your checkbook; write an autobiography or a letter; run a small business; shop from home; get the latest baseball scores or the stock report; play chess, Scrabble, or Pac-Man; compose music; create electronic art; chart your family tree; organize the household budget; book airline tickets; peruse inventories of stamp collections; and communicate electronically with other users.

Retirees are finding all kinds of uses for PCs. Al Gebber, age eighty, heads a Palm Beach computer club and has developed software to keep track of donations at the museum where he volunteers. Abe Rich, seventy-nine, spends three hours a day on his PC. "Just like other people exercise to keep in shape, I work out my mind with my computer." Esther Schneiderman, a seventy-six-year-old retired secretary living in Miami, compiled a cookbook by "chatting" electronically with other retirees (*Business Week*, September 10, 1990). Grace Young, a seventy-three-year-old widow from Belmont, California, found a cure for her sleepless nights. She logs onto a computer network that puts her in touch with people all over the country any time of the day or night. "All I have to do is to go to my computer and there's always someone to talk to, laugh with, and exchange ideas with," she says (*Wall Street Journal*, August 7, 1989).

SENIORNET

SeniorNet is a national nonprofit organization dedicated to bringing older Americans into the computer age. It was founded in 1986 by Mary Furlong with a grant from the Markle Foundation. SeniorNet currently offers computer-literacy courses to people over fifty-five at forty-two teaching sites in the US and Canada. Students receive hands-on training in computer skills at teaching sites located in schools, community centers, medical clinics, and nursing homes. Classes include basic word-processing, financial management with spreadsheets, desktop publishing, telecommunications, and "electronic citizenship," a tool for political action that uses wordprocessing to write letters expressing opinions that are mail-merged to a list of names and addresses.

SeniorNet members are linked by a national on-line computer network enabling them to communicate with each other electronically and to access information on a variety of subjects. They can send electronic mail (even love notes), hold conferences, and poll their opinions. They also receive a quarterly newsletter, discounts on hardware and software, and a free copy of their book, *Computers for Kids Over Sixty*, by Mary Furlong and Greg Kearsley. A convention is held every year, giving these electronic pen pals a chance to meet face to face.

SeniorNet
399 Arguello Boulevard
San Francisco, CA 94118
(415) 750-5030

BOOKS

Libraries, bookstores, and computer stores are filled with books covering every aspect of computing. Pick up a good basic text, such as *Computers for Kids Over Sixty* or the one mentioned below. You might also want to look at books written for children. They present the material in a simple, easy-to-follow manner using large type. Before buying a computer system, read some of the introductory books about different systems. Once you've settled on the one you want, get yourself a good guidebook to your specific system. You may also want to read a software directory to familiarize yourself with the different programs available.

The First Book of Personal Computing, by W. E. Wang and Joe Kraynak (Carmel, IN: Howard W. Sams & Co., 1990), presents an easy-to-understand, step-by-step guide to personal computing that will teach you all you need to know to get started. To keep the reader from becoming frustrated by an overload of information, it focuses on a small block of information, then builds from there. Each chapter starts with a list of topics and ends with a summary. Topics include word processing, electronic spreadsheets, computer graphics, and desktop publishing. To order, call the publisher at (800) 257-5755.

MAGAZINES

An abundance of computer magazines ranges in topics from almost any type of computer to the special needs of specific professions. Magazines can be helpful in learning about the different systems available and the many ways to use computers. They contain book reviews, informative articles, problem-solving tips, and information about conferences, user groups, and special events.

One magazine, published by the same people who publish *PC Today*, is especially geared toward beginners:

PC Novice
PO Box 85380
Lincoln, NE 68501-5380
(800) 424-7900

USER GROUPS

User groups bring together computer users so they can help one another and share common interests. They may be big or small, well organized or informal. Many groups conduct regular meetings and invite guest speakers to discuss topics of interest. Members help each other solve problems; they also share information and software. They can communicate electronically with each other using networks such as CompuServe or local bulletin boards. Your local computer store can help you locate a user group in your area, or look in *Computer Shopper* magazine for a list of user groups in the United States.

ADAPTIVE EQUIPMENT

Computer technology can be adapted to enable communication opportunities not previously possible for people with disabilities. Large-print screens and keyboards assist visually impaired individuals. Braille input and output and touch screens open up opportunities for blind people while voice input and adaptive keyboards aid people with limited mobility.

Alliance for Technology Access

The Alliance for Technology Access is a national grassroots initiative of access centers, and technology vendors working together to help people with disabilities obtain equal access to their environment through the use of technology. There are presently 46 ATA sites across the United States. Each center operates autonomously under a separate name and has its own area of expertise. For instance, one resource center specializes in the needs of people with visual impairments while another has expertise in communication disorders. At the Orlando resource center, a sixty-seven-year-old professor who was losing his sight learned computer skills that allowed him to continue teaching and doing research. Each center provides hands-on instruction-referral services and individual consultations. There are also open houses, product demonstrations, and newsletters. All ATA centers are linked electronically to each other as well as to national databases and bulletin boards through AppleLink, Apple Computer's information and communication network.

Alliance for Technology Access
National Offices
1037 Solano Avenue
Albany, CA 94706-1888
(415) 528-0747

217 Massachusetts Avenue
Lexington, MA 02173
(617) 863-9966

Techspress

Techspress is a technology-access program located at the Resource Center for Independent Living, an ATA affiliate in New York. It provides information and referral on computer-related technology services, both locally and nationwide. Techspress works with the consumer to adapt technology to their needs. It conducts monthly in-house workshops and coordinates a user group. Membership in the group includes resource library access to adaptive software, hardware, and videos, phone consultation, and a newsletter.

Techspress
Resource Center for Independent Living
409 Columbia Street
Utica, NY 13502
(315) 797-4642 (voice or TDD—Telephone Devices for the
   Deaf)

PETS

Researchers confirm what pet owners always knew. Pets are good for you. Not only do they keep you company, they keep you healthy. It has been scientifically shown that petting Fido lowers blood pressure and can actually slow the progress of stress-related diseases such as hypertension, strokes, and diabetes. Your pet doesn't even have to be warm and fuzzy to calm you down. Watching your goldfish swimming in their bowl will do the trick.

A study by Erika Friedman, associate professor of Health Science at Brooklyn College, on heart-attack patients revealed that patients who owned animals lived longer after a heart attack. Research by Judith Siegel, a psychologist and professor of health at the University of California, found that older adults who own pets visit their physicians less often. A study done at Arizona State University showed that talking to your pet can produce a short-term reduction in blood pressure.

The therapeutic benefit of animals has been demonstrated in many institutional settings. Severely withdrawn patients, physically disabled people, and autistic children often show remarkable improvement after contact with animals. People who showed no response to other kinds of treatment often became involved and communicative after stroking and playing with dogs and cats. Prisoners have become better adjusted to prison life and more open to rehabilitation through their relationship with animals.

Owning a pet can solve many of the problems inherent in retirement. The responsibility of owning a pet can give a sense of purpose and structure to your day. Smokey won't let you sleep until noon when he needs to be fed and walked. Caring for a pet fills basic nurturing needs that don't disappear when the children or grandchildren are grown. The unconditional love they give increases your self-esteem and sense of well being. Being greeted by a wagging tale when you come home combats loneliness and dissipates negative emotions. Even deep sorrows, like the loss of a spouse, can be soothed by a purring kitten or a wet nose nuzzling your lap.

Owning a pet can improve your relationships with other people and link you closer to your family. Pets give you something to share with your children and grandchildren. One retiree says that every one of her six grandchildren thinks of her dog as their own. Many therapists have discovered that communication between couples in treatment improves in the presence of the family pet. Owning a pet also increases your chances of meeting other people. A study done in London's Hyde Park found that people accompanied by their dogs spoke to more people and had longer conversations than those who walked alone.

There are, of course, disadvantages to owning pets. Travel plans and irregular schedules become a problem when you have an animal to care for. Furniture and rugs are not always safe from the most well behaved critters. Yet pet owners believe that the joy pets bring to their lives is worth kitty hair collecting in the corners and morning walks in the rain. After all, who else will listen attentively to your stories and complaints without judging you or putting in their own two cents?

Determining which animal is right for you will depend on your personal preferences and lifestyle. Some people prefer to adopt a grown dog to avoid the trouble of housebreaking. To others, happiness is a warm puppy. Cats don't need to be housebroken. Their mom teaches them how to use the litter box, but kittens can be quite mischievous. Be sure you have the patience to wait out their energetic childhood before bringing a kitten home. (Remember to put the china in a closed cabinet! Climbing and knocking things down is one of their favorite games.) Cats don't have to be walked and can be left alone most of the day with fresh water and food. If they are left longer than accustomed, however, they have ways of letting you know they are angry. The myth that cats are aloof and unaffectionate is not true. They are experts at giving and receiving love, though of course it must be on their own terms. If protection is a consideration, you might want a large dog, but if you don't like getting yanked around, choose a smaller breed. Little lap dogs can be constant companions. You can take them with you wherever you go. Caring for the smaller breeds, however, often involves expensive grooming. If you are on a fixed income, this may be a consideration.

Countless animals need a loving home. Every year 10 million animals are destroyed simply because there is no one to care for them. Finding a pet should be easy and inexpensive. Almost every community has an ASPCA or Humane Society that provides adoption services and veterinary care. Even if you can't keep a pet at home, you can still gain some of the advantages of relating to animals by volunteering to walk or play with the animals at the shelter. If you are over sixty, the Ralston Purina company will match you up with a pet free of charge, arrange for a complete health checkup—including all necessary shots and spaying or neutering—and provide a starter kit of food, supplies, and a booklet on how to care for your pet. For an application, write:

Purina Pets for People Program
Checkerboard Square
St. Louis, MO 63164

GARDENING

Gardening connects us to the roots of life. The gardener's material is alive. His instruments are the elements earth, air, and water. His medium is the cycle of growth and decline. His relationship to his garden is one between living entities. A gardener learns to work in cooperation with nature, which flourishes under his tending but will not be dominated. A garden is never static; it is constantly changing. It is never finished, but is always in process. The fruits of a gardeners' labor are plain to see and his plans for the future are always evolving. A gardener grows more than plants and flowers; he grows hope and regenerates himself.

The rejuvenating aspects of gardening are confirmed by research. Studies by Roger Ulrich, an associate professor of geography at the University of Delaware, show that exposure to plants results in lower blood pressure, slower heart rate, and relaxed muscles. Not only does gardening lower stress and provide a sense of well-being and satisfaction, it is also an excellent low-impact workout, mixing different types of movements, stretching and toning both upper and lower body and burning calories.

Gardening is the number one leisure activity in the country. Fifty million Americans garden. It is not necessary to own a plot of land to enjoy gardening. House plants keep your home free of pollutants and fill the need to nurture growing things. Many community groups, such as the Boston Urban Gardeners, turn vacant lots in inner cities into gardens tended by interested citizens. Community gardens provide opportunities not only to enrich yourself but contribute to the quality of life in your neighborhood. In the Elmhurst section of Queens, New York, which suffers all the blights of a changing urban environment, a spot of beauty mocks the dreariness of its surroundings and reminds the inhabitants of the tenacity of nature. The garden adorns the public library and is tended by the neighborhood seniors. They may not always be aware of the joy they provide those who pass by, but their labors do give hope to those who do not have the luxury of tending their own gardens.

A visit to your local library or bookstore will uncover volumes on the subject. There are clubs, classes, museums, magazines, and catalogues on every type of garden.

AMERICAN HORTICULTURAL SOCIETY

The American Horticultural Society, founded in 1922, is dedicated to excellence in horticulture. It seeks to educate both amateurs and professionals on how to obtain the best results for themselves and for the environment. Members receive *American Horticulturist* magazine and *American Horticulture News Edition* and have access to a gardener's helpline, which answers all gardening questions toll free. Membership includes discounts on books, a free seed program, travel opportunities, and workshops and lectures at their headquarters in Washington DC.

American Horticultural Society
7931 East Boulevard Drive
Alexandria, VA 22308
(800) 777-7931

BROOKLYN BOTANIC GARDEN

The Brooklyn Botanic Garden is one outstanding example of the many beautiful public gardens around the country. Its fifty-two acres contain a diversity of plant specimens and garden styles. The Japanese gardens that surround a lake inhabited by colorful fish and ducks is a favorite of visitors, as are the herb garden and lily ponds. Classes, lectures, and tours are held throughout the year. A subscribing member of the Brooklyn Botanic Garden receives *Plant and Gardens* magazine and a new quarterly *Plant and Garden* handbook covering more than fifty gardening topics, from beds and borders to weed control. Members are also entitled to a plant information service by phone or mail. For a catalogue of available books and membership information, contact:

Brooklyn Botanic Garden
1000 Washington Avenue
Brooklyn, NY 11225
(718) 622-4433

CONTAINER GARDENING

Neither limited space nor limited mobility need impair your ability to garden. Container gardening can turn a rooftop, patio, balcony, or window into a blooming haven. Raised beds make it possible for people in wheelchairs or of limited mobility to garden in a comfortable sitting position. The following sources can provide information on container and raised-bed gardening:

Container Gardening
Sunset Series
Lane Magazine and Book
  Company
Menlo Park, CA 94025
(415) 321-3600

Container Gardening
Brooklyn Botanic Garden
100 Washington Avenue
Brooklyn, NY 11225
(718) 622-4433

Gardening in Raised Beds and
  Container Gardening
  for the Elderly and
  Handicapped
Department of Horticulture
Virginia Polytechnic Institute
  and State University
Blacksburg, VA 24061
(703) 231-5451

The Wheelabout Garden
The National Easter Seal
  Society
2023 West Ogden Avenue
Chicago, IL 60612
(312) 939-5115

BOOKS AND OTHER PUBLICATIONS

Gardening by Mail, by Barbara Barton (Boston: Hougton Mifflin, 1990), is the definitive resource on resources. This mail-order directory contains thousands of sources on everything for the garden and gardener, including seed companies, nurseries, supplies, ornaments, horticultural and plant societies, magazines, libraries, and books. If you can't find it in your local library or bookstore, contact the publisher:

Houghton Mifflin Company
Wayside Road
Burlington, MA 01803
(617) 272-1500

GARDENER'S SUPPLY

The Gardener's Supply Catalogue is filled with innovative solutions for gardening problems such as the easy kneeler, a sturdy, lightweight frame that lets you lower yourself down for clipping or weeding and push yourself up again without straining your back; upside down, it becomes a bench. Ratchet-action hand prunes will cut a half-inch hardwood branch with very little hand strength, and the lightweight yard cart makes hauling topsoil or garden tools easy. The catalogue includes tools, supplies, furniture, seeds, and many more products to meet the needs of indoor and outdoor gardeners and to help protect the environment.

Gardener's Supply
128 Intervale Road
Burlington, VT 05401
(800) 457-4031

GreenPrints is a quarterly magazine that won't tell you how to do anything. Its concern is not the technique, but the spirit of gardening, the gardener's relationship to his garden, the joys and sorrows of a gardener's experience. It includes beautifully written poems and essays filled with philosophy and humor that express the personal connection between people and plants.

GreenPrints
PO Box 1355
Fairview, NC 28730
(704) 628-1902

CHAPTER V

Second Careers

"It might be kind of a relief to be finished. It's sort of like you don't know what kind of a yard dash you're running, but then you're at the finish line and you sort of sigh—you've made it! But you never have— you have to start all over again."

MARILYN MONROE

For many retirees, there is no substitute for paid work. They're just not happy unless they are working. Others need to work to supplement their pensions or to be able to afford their leisure interests. In any case, retirement careers differ from pre-retirement careers. Most involve greater choice and flexibility and are less stressful and demanding. Even if retirees must work to meet financial obligations, their expenses are lower than those of a growing family, and there is already a basis of support from Social Security, pensions, and investments. There are many alternatives to the traditional nine-to-five approach to work. Flex time, job sharing, consulting, phased retirement, and part-time, temporary, and seasonal work all offer ways to enjoy the benefits of work at a more relaxed pace.

157

Second careers can provide an opportunity to do work you enjoy. Starting your own business, turning a hobby into a career, or finally doing the kind of work you always wanted are possibilities. Work has a different meaning now. You don't have to make a killing or climb up the corporate ladder. You can work for whatever personal benefits you deem important. Some retirees choose to take jobs with less prestige than their first careers had because they enjoy the benefits of work but don't want the stress or responsibility they once had. They might take a lesser position at their old company or choose another type of job altogether, such as doorman or security guard. "I used to be purchasing manager for a bank. Then I retired, and in six months I'd done everything I'd been planning for the last thirty years, so I wanted to work again," Bill Kramlinger told the *New York Times*. At age sixty-seven, he went to work as a courier at the Minnesota Tile Company in Minneapolis, where retirees working in pairs staff the entire courier department. "I work half the month and I look forward to a few weeks off while my partner works. Then, when I'm getting bored, it's time to come back (*New York Times*, April 22, 1990).

Finding suitable work presents challenges for everyone. Difficult economic times and prejudice against older workers can present further barriers. But older workers have many assets that can overcome these difficulties. They bring with them the experience, skills, and knowledge of a lifetime. Most older workers have a strong work ethic that makes them excellent employees. They take pride in the quality of their work and are loyal and dependable. Their productivity level is high. They have fewer accidents and their attendance records are equal to or better than those of younger employees. Their average length of stay on one job is fifteen years.

The myth that a worker's value diminishes with age is simply not true. The kinds of work performed today, the modernization of the workplace, and improved health of older citizens have removed the limitations once associated with aging workers. Most jobs today require interpersonal skills, sound judgment, and specialized knowledge rather than brute strength. Eyeglasses and hearing aids compensate for sensory deterioration. Computerization makes many jobs safer and easier. Air-conditioning and central heating make the workplace more comfortable, and shorter work days and work weeks means physical stamina is not a requirement for high performance.

Some futurists believe older workers will soon be highly sought by employers looking to fill empty slots. They predict that the "baby bust" generation that followed the "baby boomers" will not be able to supply enough workers to fill needed positions and that a changing society will require many new kinds of jobs not yet imagined. In the last decade, the outlook for older workers has greatly improved. Prominent figures such as Ronald Reagan and Lee Iacocca have done much to demonstrate the capabilities of older people.

Some companies already tap this labor resource. It is not unusual for top executives to be called back on a consulting basis to assist in launching new projects or during peak periods. Travelers Insurance in Hartford, Connecticut, operates a job bank that not only recruits retirees from its own company but other companies as well to fill part-time and temporary positions. Universities seek retired businesspeople and specialists as teachers. The "McMasters Program" trains and places people fifty-five and over in McDonalds across the country. Walt Disney World recruits retirees to staff their park. Days Inn actively seeks retirees to work as reservation agents, desk clerks, and managers. Yet the demand for returning retirees is still relatively small and discrimination against older workers remains a problem. Retirees wishing to begin a second career must be creative, flexible, and persistent.

JOB SEARCH STRATEGIES

The first step in any successful job search is to analyze your goals, needs, assets, and limitations. What do you want your job to accomplish? Are you looking for challenge, social interaction, or opportunities to be of service? Do you need to earn a certain amount of money? Be specific about how much pay you require, how much time you wish to commit, and what kind of work environment you prefer. Keep in mind there is an earning limit for people under seventy who wish to keep their full Social Security benefits. To find out how this affects you, call or visit your local Social Security office, or call the Social Security information line at (800) 234-5772.

When you have a clear idea of what you want from your job, take an honest assessment of what you have to offer. What are your skills? What experience do you have? Do you have specialized knowledge in a particular field? Consider all the qualifications you have, not just on-the-job skills. Did you organize your club's fundraising event? Have you kept books for the block association? Do you repair the broken appliances in your home? Allow yourself to brainstorm. You'll find you have more assets than you realized.

Next consider your limitations. Do you have any medical conditions that need to be taken into account? Must you work close to home? Are you only available certain hours of the day? Do you need the stimulus of other workers or do you work best alone?

Now consider the types of jobs you can do. Look at as broad a range of occupations as you can. Looking at too narrow a picture will greatly limit your prospects. Be flexible. You may not find the exact kind of position you are looking for or had before.

Once you have an idea of what you want, research the field. The public library is a good place to start. You will find an

abundance of resource material available to you. Trade magazines and journals can provide information on specific fields
and often list job openings. There are reference guides and
directories to associations, publications, and industries. Reference books such as *Standard and Poor's Register of Corporations*
provide company profiles, including names and addresses of
officers and department heads. *The Occupational Outlook Handbook*
has information on jobs, training, salary scales, and opportunities in hundreds of occupations. *The Wall Street Journal* puts out
The National Business Employment Weekly, which contains articles
of help to job seekers and listings of employment opportunities. Education and Job Information Centers (EJIC) are located in public libraries in every state. They offer such services as
computerized job banks, career counseling, job training information, testing, and up-to-date listings of job openings.

Talk to other people who have similar positions. Call up the
organization you're interested in or a similar one and ask if
someone could spend a few minutes discussing the field with
you. Since you are asking only for information, not for work,
at this point most people will be glad to make time for you.
What you learn at this interview will provide invaluable information on how to apply for the work you want. You may also
discover that it really wasn't what you wanted to do at all and
save yourself a lot of time and trouble.

An assessment of the job market should include more than
looking in the want ads. You could start by asking your former
employer if they employ retirees on a part-time, temporary, or
consultant basis. Consult your state employment service and
area agency on aging. Ask friends and relatives. Join business
associations and network. Look around your neighborhood
for ways to use your skills. If you decide to register with a
private employment agency, be sure they're looking out for
you, not just trying to fill positions.

You will need a résumé. It is your calling card and should

represent you in the best possible light. At the same time it must be a true assessment of your experience and not be an idealized version of yourself. Potential employers are good at spotting fabrications and exaggerations. Don't put in everything you ever did. A good résumé should highlight the most important aspects of your experience in one page. Be specific when explaining duties. "Responsible for overall supervision of department" doesn't tell them anything. "Hired staff of twenty-one instructors. Coordinated budget of $40,000," does. The appearance of your résumé is as important as the content. It must be neat and readable. Be sure there are no spelling or grammatical errors.

A cover letter should accompany each résumé you send. In no more than a few paragraphs, let your potential employer know that you have some knowledge of their organization, have a specific reason for wanting to work for them, and suggest ways you can assist them. End the letter with a request for an interview and let them know you will follow up with a phone call.

Once you have an interview scheduled, prepare carefully. You should have some idea of the company's goals, policies, strengths, and weaknesses in order to convince them of your value to them. Be meticulous in your grooming. Appearance does count. Dress as closely as possible to the organization's code for the position. Arrive a few minutes early so you can observe and adjust to your environment. During the interview relax and be yourself. Project energy and confidence. Keep in mind that your interviewers may be as uncomfortable as you are in these situations and do what you can to keep them at their ease.

Outplacement specialist James E. Challenger warns against "becoming your own worst enemy by bringing negative baggage to the interview." Highlighting accomplishments that took place years ago (possibly before your interviewer was born) such as your record in World War II, send the message that you are focused on the past, not the future. Dressing dowdy, rumpled, or out of style is another turn off. Emphasizing that you retired early or only plan to work a limited amount of time gives the impression that work is secondary to you. Instead of letting your age work against you, use it to your advantage. Stress your experience. It's your best asset. "Sell expertise that the company wants at that moment. Be ready to cite specific examples of how you helped improve profitability, efficiency, or company recognition (*Wall Street Journal*, December 4, 1989).

Not only does your prospective employer need to learn about you before making a decision, you need to learn about them before making yours. Though it is not considered good policy to discuss salary at the first interview, it does need to be settled before accepting the job. You also need to know about benefits, sick leave, and vacation policies. Learn as much as you can about what is expected of you before making a commitment.

Looking for a job is a job itself. Employment counselors suggest you treat it as such and spend no less than thirty-five hours a week on your search. It could take many months before you find what you want. Mr. Challenger, the outplacement specialist, estimates that the average job search for someone over sixty takes two to three months longer than someone ten years their junior. With persistence and an optimistic attitude, you should eventually succeed. There are many places to turn for help. The employment office of your state's Department of Labor and your local area's agency on aging can point you in the right direction. Libraries and bookstores have shelves of information on how to conduct a search, write a résumé, and present a successful image. The following sources have proven helpful to many people.

AARP WORKS

AARP WORKS helps mid-life and older persons develop effective job-search techniques. An eight-week workshop helps participants redefine their skills, interests, and work experience in order to find jobs that meet their needs and abilities. AARP WORKS has demonstrated its effectiveness. A follow-up study of participants over a fifteen-month period found that 71 percent of those actively looking for work obtained job interviews. For information on an AARP WORKS site near you, write:

AARP WORKS
Work Force Education
Worker Equity Department
601 E Street NW
Washington, DC 20049

Forty-Plus Clubs

40-Plus Clubs helps older executives, managers, and professionals find new jobs or start new careers. Since its inception in 1939, it has helped more than 50,000 members nationwide find the right job. Their training programs focus on the skills and techniques of a successful job search, rebuilding self-esteem, restoring confidence, and motivating members to achieve success. There are seventeen Forty-Plus chapters around the country. To locate the one nearest you, consult your local telephone directory.

Publications

What Color is Your Parachute?, by Richard Bolls (Berkeley: Ten Speed Press, updated annually), is a classic in its field. A "Practical Guide for Job-Hunters and Career-Changers" remains the definitive "how to" for anyone entering or re-entering the job market or changing fields. It will take you step-by-step through the process of finding a job while entertaining and encouraging you along the way. Most bookstores carry it; you can also look for it in the library or order it from the publisher.

Ten Speed Press
Box 7123
Berkeley, CA 94707
(415) 845-8414

"Working Options: How to Plan Your Job Search, Your Work Life" is an AARP brochure designed to encourage you to reach your employment goals. It addresses the specific needs of older job seekers and outlines a step-by-step approach to a successful self-directed job search. To obtain a copy, send a request to the address below. Include the title and AARP publication number, D12403 to:

AARP Fulfillment
601 E Street NW
Washington, DC 20049

Starting Over: You in the New Workplace, by Jo Danna (Briarwood, NY: Palomino Press, 1990), is a comprehensive guidebook for career and job changers that is especially useful to retirees wishing to re-enter the job market. It not only provides practical information on how to find work in today's changing world but deals with the psychological adjustment to rapid technological and social change as well.

Palomino Press
86-07 144th Street
Briarwood, NY 11435
(718) 297-5053

JOB-TRAINING AND PLACEMENT PROGRAMS

Technological changes over the past twenty-five years have revamped the way work is done and created new kinds of jobs. Home computers have opened up innumerable options for running your own business. An increase in service jobs have brought new opportunities for employment. Learning the skills required in today's market can be an excellent way to re-enter the work force.

There are many ways to acquire new skills or brush up on old ones. Continuing-education programs at universities, high schools, and community centers offer an abundance of courses in job-related subjects. Many home-study programs are designed to teach vocational skills. Vocational training schools exist in almost every community, and government programs serve special needs. Following are several training and placement programs you might find helpful. (See also Chapter III, Lifelong Learning, for more job-training resources.)

HOME-STUDY SCHOOLS

Home-study programs offer training in many kinds of career opportunities. They can prepare you for work in areas that welcome retirees, such as the travel and hotel/motel industries and paralegal professions. You can turn your hobby into a career with courses in landscaping, floristry, dressmaking, and doll technology. Contact the Home Study Council for a list of accredited home-study schools.

National Home Study Council
1601 Eighteenth Street NW
Washington, DC 20009
(202) 234-5100

Job Training Partnership Act (JTPA)

The Job Training Partnership Act establishes federally funded job-training and placement programs for economically disadvantaged adults fifty-five and over. It is administered by each state in conjunction with the private sector. Older workers receive such services as job-search assistance, job development, and job training to prepare for employment with private business concerns. For further information, contact your state's Office on the Aging, listed in your telephone directory.

Senior Community Service Employment Program (SCSEP)

The Senior Community Service Employment Program, established under the Older Americans Act of 1965, is funded by the Department of Labor and administered by ten national senior advocacy organizations in conjunction with each state. People fifty-five and over with limited incomes work in temporary positions in nonprofit and public agencies in order to develop the skills and experience necessary to obtain permanent employment. All positions pay at least minimum wage. Participants receive on-the-job training as well as job-search and placement assistance. Typical jobs include bookkeeper, day-care worker, mechanic, receptionist, data-entry clerk, and groundskeeper. For further information, contact your state's Office on the Aging.

Senior Environmental Employment Program (AARP/SEE Program)

AARP, in conjunction with the Environmental Protection Agency, established a program that puts the skills, talents, and experience of older Americans to work. Participants assist the EPA in short-term paid assignments, ranging from clerical to highly technical positions. Benefits include sick leave, paid vacations and holidays, health insurance, and a one-year complimentary AARP membership. For information on enrolling with SEE, write:

AARP/Senior Environmental Employment Program
601 E Street NW
Washington, DC 20049

STARTING YOUR OWN BUSINESS

If you've dreamed of owning your own business, retirement could be the perfect opportunity to realize your ambitions. With your pension and Social Security as a base of support, you won't starve through the initial start-up, which could take two years or more, and you can more comfortably weather the inevitable ups and downs of establishing a business. You have the time to concentrate your efforts and the knowledge and experience of a lifetime to draw from.

Not everyone has the temperament of an entrepreneur. If you want to work a limited amount of time, prefer following direction to decision-making, or need the security of a steady paycheck, don't go into business for yourself. Starting a business is risky. According to the Small Business Administration, three out of four businesses fail in the first year of operation and nine out of ten fail within ten years.

If you have the entrepreneurial spirit, you'll be willing to take this risk. You'll have the drive and persistence to keep going when things get tough. Failures will be perceived as opportunities to learn. You'll take charge of the situation and allow your creative thinking to overcome the obstacles. You won't quit until you've reached your goal. Above all, you'll believe in yourself and your ability to succeed.

Taking time to research your market and learn the ins and

outs of running a small business before jumping in will help you avoid some of the pitfalls. There is much help available. A trip to your local library or bookstore will uncover many resources. Your local chamber of commerce and Small Business Administration can provide invaluable information.

SMALL BUSINESS ADMINISTRATION (SBA)

The Small Business Administration has many ways to help you get started in your own business. A toll-free call to their answer desk [(800) 827-5722)] will provide information on how to establish a business plan, how to obtain financing, including SBA loans, and where to get training. They'll send you a start-up kit with a list of over fifty available publications, planning guides, and other valuable information.

Small Business Development Centers (SBDCs) are located in every state, generally situated near colleges or universities. They offer management assistance, training, and counseling. The Service Corps of Retired Executives (SCORE) provide counseling and free advice as well as workshops on how to start a business. (See page 39).

PUBLICATIONS

How to Start a Profitable Retirement Business, by Arthur Liebers (Babylon, NY: Pilot Books, 1987), offers many suggestions for retirement businesses, such as pet care, newspaper clipping, handyman services, management consulting, and mail-order and franchised businesses. It also contains a checklist for going into business.

Pilot Books, Inc.
103 Cooper Street
Babylon, NY 11702
(516) 422-2225

Think and Grow Rich, by Napoleon Hill (New York: Fawcett Crest, 1960), is a classic positive-thinking text that has helped many entrepreneurs develop the motivation, drive, and self-confidence necessary to achieve their goals. It reveals "the law of success" derived from the combined experience of great achievers such as Andrew Carnegie and Thomas Edison. Learn how to make this secret formula work for you. Most bookstores carry *Think and Grow Rich*; you may also look for it in your library or order it from the publisher.

Random House
400 Hahn Road
Westminster, MD 21157
(800) 733-3000

The following government publications are available from the Superintendent of Documents: "Starting and Managing a Small Business of Your Own," "Buying and Selling a Small Business," and "Starting and Managing a Small Business from Your Home." To order, write to:

Superintendent of Documents
Government Printing Office
Washington, DC 20402
(202) 783-3238

CHAPTER VI

The Arts

"I see little of more importance to the future of our country and our civilization than full recognition of the place of the artist."

JOHN F. KENNEDY
Amherst College
October 26, 1963

Art is food for the soul. It delights our senses and brings meaning to our world. It is a mirror in which we see ourselves and others reflected in different lights. It is said that art is the only thing that lasts. We know of past civilizations through their art, and we will be known by the art we leave behind. Art seeks the truth, no matter how painful, and though it demands the best of us, it is within the reach of anyone. It belongs to all of us. Leisure provides the environment in which it may flourish. Those who possess leisure may also possess art.

Too often people limit their self-expression by thinking art is something beyond reach. You don't have to be Picasso to paint. Knowing you will never dance with the New York City Ballet should not stop you from being the best dancer you can be. Testing yourself to your limits is gratifying whatever your skill level. Age is no limit. Grandma Moses did not begin painting until she was past seventy. Titian painted his master-piece, *The Battle of Lepanto*, at the age of ninety-eight. If Marlee Matlin, a hearing- and speech-impaired actress, can obtain Hollywood's highest honor, the Academy Award, there can be no doubt of the ability of disabled persons to achieve excel-lence in any chosen art form.

The concept of talent is often misunderstood. Though no one knows where talent comes from or who may be the one to possess it, only hard work and dedication make talent bloom. How do you know what potential you have until you explore your capabilities? Why not be like the four-year-old who, when asked if she could play the piano, replied, "I don't know. I never tried."

Elizabeth Layton was sixty-eight when she discovered her hidden talent. A homemaker from Wellsville, Kansas, she suffered depression most of her life. Neither psychotherapy, drugs, nor electroshock therapy was able to cure her. Then she enrolled in a drawing class and changed her life. "I found a mission," she said. "All my life I remember being sad, even when I was a kid. That's a part of depression. Then, one day, I was working on a drawing and all at once it hit me. I wasn't depressed anymore." Her talent was immediately recognized by her teacher and a local newspaper reporter who showed her work to museums. After appearing in exhibits in Wichita, Kansas City, and at the Mid-American Arts Alliance, her one-woman show toured the country.

Ms. Layton's drawings make powerful statements about such poignant subjects as the holocaust, racial bigotry, and AIDS. "I decided that if I had been given the know-how to draw, I needed to use it for a purpose," she says (*Parade*, May 28, 1989).

Opportunities for participating in and appreciating art are

abundant. Museums, theaters, concerts, amateur groups, classes, seminars, workshops, and tours provide ample occasions for exploring culture. Discounts and free tickets are often available to older people for many kinds of cultural events. For information on cultural opportunities in your community, contact your local mayor's office, arts council, or area agency on aging.

THE NATIONAL CENTER ON THE ARTS AND AGING (NCAA)

NCAA is a program of the National Council on the Aging, Inc. It is the only national program to exclusively address arts and aging issues. With the assistance of the National Endowment for the Arts and individual corporate donors, the center works toward involving older adults in the arts as participants, volunteers, patrons, and audiences.

NCAA's resource and information center serves as a clearinghouse for information on arts and aging issues. It provides consultation and technical services, disseminates technical materials and publications, and maintains a library of arts and aging literature. The center also conducts workshops and conferences and contributes regularly to publications in the arts and aging fields.

The Arts Mentor Program trains older artists as teachers, workshop leaders, and artists-in-residence in community settings serving children and adults. It also provides technical assistance to those wishing to implement such a project in new locations.

Located in the foyer of the National Council on the Aging, one block from the Smithsonian, Gallery Patina is devoted exclusively to exhibiting fine arts and crafts by older artists. Both established and emerging artists are showcased. Works by older artists are also exhibited in traveling exhibitions and joint exhibitions with major museum and galleries across the United States.

The Resource Guide to People, Places, and Programs in Arts and Aging, published by the National Council on the Arts, contains a comprehensive listing of national and state programs serving older adults. It contains program profiles and contact sources and may be obtained by contacting the Council.

National Center on Arts and Aging
West Wing 100
600 Maryland Avenue SW
Washington, DC 20024
(202) 479-1200

ACCESS TO ART

Blindness or visual impairment need not prohibit participation in the visual arts. The American Foundation for the Blind, in conjunction with the Museum of American Folk Art, compiled a museum directory of several hundred museums, historical societies, and other facilities across the US that provide services for blind and visually impaired people. To obtain a copy of the booklet "Access to Art," write:

American Foundation for the Blind
15 West 16th Street
New York, NY 10011
(800) 232-5463

DANCE

The impulse to express ourselves through rhythmic body movement is a universal human trait. Nearly all people dance. From the ancient campfire to the modern disco, dance has been woven into the cultures of nearly all societies. We dance to celebrate important occasions and rites of passage, to preserve the traditions of our homeland or our subculture, to meet and court, to appreciate the wonder of the human body, and to experience the joy of movement. It does our souls good to dance.

Dance is an enjoyable way to remain active, fit, and involved with others. The notion that dance belongs to highly trained, youthful bodies is proven wrong every day at classes, dances, and performances in every American community. It is never too late to learn to dance. Ruth Katherine Spargur, a retired beautician from Indianapolis, first put on her tap shoes at age eighty-four. She always wanted to dance, but her late husband thought "dancing was undignified." When she attended a tapdance recital of one of her eleven great-grandchildren, she decided it was time to realize her dreams. Being seventy years older than the other students didn't stop her from enrolling in class. She has since won first place in the over-fifty category in two Indianapolis dance contests and is in constant demand by local TV stations, senior centers, and school recitals.

DANCE RESOURCE GUIDE

The National Dance Association, with data from the National Arts Education Research Center at the University of Illinois, has compiled a resource guide to dance music, recording companies, books, journals, organizations, and multicultural resources. For mail order information, contact:

American Alliance for Health, Physical Education, Recreation, and Dance
1900 Association Drive
Reston, VA 22091
(703) 476-3436

THE DANCE EXCHANGE

"There is no reason why the prevailing attitude in this country couldn't be... 'when I retire I'm going to become a dancer,'" says Liz Lerman, artistic director and founder of the Dance Exchange. Her two companies, Dancers of the Third Age and Liz Lerman/Exchange, shatter traditional concepts of what dance is and who dancers are. Members of Dancers of the Third Age range in age from sixty to ninety. Like Carolyn Rosenthal, most have never danced professionally before. "I used to be a watcher," she explains. "When I lived in New York, I used to go to all the dance concerts, but I realized I never 'owned' my body." Then she met Ms. Lerman and at the age of sixty became a performer (*Washington Weekly*, July 9, 1984).

Dancers of the Third Age have appeared at elementary schools, universities, art galleries, senior residences, national conventions, seminars, and festivals across the United States and in Europe. They have performed at the Smithsonian Institution, Wolf Trap Farm Park for the Performing Arts, the Spoleto Festival, the National Council on Aging, and Scensommar 85 in Stockholm, Sweden. The group is the subject of the Metromedia TV special, "I Don't Feel Old When I'm Dancing."

Dancers of the Third Age often join members of Liz Lerman/ Exchange, a modern dance group comprised of young professional dancers, to present pieces that mesh with the movements of older and younger dancers. Their dances explore issues such as the relationship between fathers and sons and the memories of grandmothers and mothers. Only an older performer has the power and presence to reveal a lifetime of experience through movement. Their work has been acclaimed not only for its uniqueness of concept, but also because it belies the notion that real dance is the exclusive domain of youth.

To implement the philosophy that dance belongs to everyone, the Dance Exchange offers performances and classes in a wide variety of settings around the Washington, DC, area, including community centers, hospitals, nursing homes, senior centers, and prisons. They offer teacher-training courses and assistance to others wishing to implement similar programs in their communities. For further information about the Dance Exchange, including performance schedules, contact:

Dance Exchange, Inc.
1746B Kalorama Road NW
Washington, DC 20009
(202) 232-0833

COUNTRY DANCE AND SONG SOCIETY

The Country Dance and Song Society is dedicated to the preservation, enjoyment, study, and teaching of traditional English and American dance music and song. Its members include recreational dancers, musicians, singers, teachers, callers, and dance historians. The society's interests focus on social and participatory dance forms, including contra, squares, reels, clog, English country dance, and related music. The organization provides a referral service with information about events and historical and regional aspects of dance and music. It offers workshops, consultations, and leadership training across the country. It publishes newsletters and an annual magazine. The society also maintains a reference library and sales department through which recordings, books, videos, and other material may be purchased by mail.

Their summer workshops at Pinewoods in Massachusetts and Buffalo Gap in West Virginia provide opportunities to learn and participate in traditional dance forms amid natural splendor. Sessions run for one week. Daytime workshops offer topics that range from English and American dance to folk music. Evening dances include skits, singing, and parties. Most accommodations are in double-occupancy cabins with bathroom facilities close by. Single rooms and houses with a variety of rooms are also available.

Dance has always been important to Rita Kaplin, a seventy-year-old retired social worker from New York. She studied ballet from the age of three through her teens. Then, a few years before retiring, she discovered the fun of English country and contra dance. Since retiring, she devotes more time to dancing and is active in her local country-dance group. She attends weekly dance sessions where new dances are taught; Saturday-night dances featuring different callers and bands; and special balls complete with period costumes. Dancers of all ages and ability turn out for these events. What Rita most enjoys about this style of dancing is that in each dance she interacts not only with her partner but with seven or eight other couples.

The Country Dance and Song Society can help you locate a country dance group in your area. You may contact them at:

Country Dance and Song Society
17 New South Street
Northampton, MA 01060
(413) 584-9913

National Square Dance Directory

The *National Square Dance Directory* lists more than 10,000 square, round, contra, clogging, and folk dance clubs throughout the world. It also provides information on festivals, conventions, square dance callers, records, equipment, clothing, publications, and organizations.

National Square Dance Directory
PO Box 54055
Jackson, MS 39288
(800) 542-4010

BALLROOM DANCE

Ballroom dancing isn't coming back. It never left. For over fifty years, couples have been fox trotting and jitterbugging to the big-band sound in ballrooms all across America. The young generation, discovering the joys of couple dancing for the first time, share the floor with veterans who never stopped moving to their favorite beat. Some of the old bands still perform, and new bands play the same old swing-and-sway music. If ballroom is new to you, you'll find classes at community centers, YWCAs, and dance schools in almost any community. If you haven't danced since the kids were born, what are you waiting for? It's a great way to have fun and stay fit. Lack of a partner shouldn't keep you away. Ballrooms are still great places to make friends and find romance.

Carol Berthrong, a retired school counselor from Marshalltown, Indiana, and Beryl Peavey, a retired university professor living in Louisville, Kentucky, had their first date and first dance together in the University Ballroom in the 1930s to the music of Jan Garber. They lost track of each other, but met again at their fiftieth class reunion. Inspired by being together again, they wrote a song entitled "Finding Our Song," and some fifty years after their first dance danced to their song played by the Jan Garber Orchestra.

US Amateur Ballroom Dancer Association (USABDA)

The USABDA is a national organization unifying numerous amateur ballroom dance groups around the country. It conducts events and dances, including National Dance Week, which promotes special events across the country. Championships are held each year to select couples to represent the United States at the Ballroom World Championships. *Amateur Dancers*, a national newsletter, keeps members up-to-date on dance events. The USABDA can put you in touch with dance groups in your area. For information, contact:

USABDA
8102 Glen Gary Road
Baltimore, MD 21234
(800) 447-9047

Dancing USA

Dancing USA is a national magazine devoted to ballroom and big-band enthusiasts. It will keep you up-to-date on orchestras, ballrooms, and dance events across the country. You'll learn where to get the latest dance videos, books, and dance shoes, as well as where to dance to your favorite music anywhere in the country.

Dancing USA
10600 University Avenue NW
Minneapolis, MN 55433-6166
(612) 757-4414

DRAMA

Since the dawn of civilization, people have dramatized their experiences in order to communicate and come to terms with the human condition. Drama provides a means of transcending our limits and exploring the mysteries of our world. No other art form can create the immediacy of theater, where actor and audience share the belief that life is unfolding before them.

Drama is a collaborative art requiring the efforts of actors, directors, producers, set designers, costume designers, stage managers, stage hands, lighting specialists, sound technicians, ushers, house managers, box office help, and audiences to make the magic happen. Each one of these areas is full of opportunities for involvement. If you like to perform, work backstage, raise money, sew costumes, or sit back and enjoy the show, you can find many ways to participate. Theater groups operated by and for older adults are springing up all over the country. Many nonprofit community theaters rely on volunteer assistance to survive and need your help in all aspects of production. Discounts and free tickets are often available to older adults, and theater arts are taught at community centers and schools across the country.

THEATRICAL VOLUNTEERS

Volunteers participate in every aspect of production. They raise money, sell refreshments at intermission, paint sets, take tickets, sew costumes, and perform. An excellent way to see free theater is volunteering to usher. Most local theaters rely on volunteer ushers and will welcome your help.

At Arena Stage in Washington, DC, volunteers are called "Angels." Carmen Gowers, sixty-five, donates one day a week. "They rely on us so much," he says. "They give us special-appreciation lunches, and we get complimentary tickets to the performances. But the real reward is knowing that you're doing something important for your community. Small theaters don't make much money. Without volunteers, they probably couldn't survive."

"I've always loved the theater," says Binnie Brooks, sixty-three, who volunteers at the Old Globe Theater in San Diego where she used to take her children to see plays. "I'm not a frustrated performer, but I am star-struck. I love to meet the actors and actresses."

If you love the theater, there are many ways to take part. For information on volunteer opportunities in your community, contact your local council on the arts, community theater, college, community center, or area office on aging.

AN ACTOR'S CRAFT

Almost everyone sometime has imagined being a star of stage or screen. If the desire to act burns in you, why not follow your passion? It isn't necessary to win an Academy Award before you can reap the joys of performing. Many amateur groups provide an outlet for the secret star in all of us. Who knows? Maybe you do have the talent to become a great artist and all you need is belief in yourself and a willingness to perfect your skills. It's never too late to learn to act.

Billie Berman raised three children and worked as a micro-biology teacher most of her life. One day, the children were grown, her husband had died, and her six-bedroom house had just burned to the ground. She sat down and wrote a list of things she had never done. On that list was the word actress. It was just an idea she always had. She thought, "What do I have to lose?"

At the age of fifty-seven, she moved to New York and rented a one-room apartment. "The Murphy bed collapsed into the one wall, and the kitchen collapsed into the other wall. The only thing that didn't collapse was the toilet. I didn't care." She took acting classes, received a call back at her very first audition, and two years later landed a role at the Actor's Theater of Louisville. At sixty-eight she's going strong. She wrote and performed her own one-woman show, "Really? You Don't Look Like One!" at the New England Repertory, Alabama Shakespeare, and Riverside Shakespeare theaters (*Backstage*, May 2, 1990).

"Theater keeps you buoyant, hopeful, dreamy-eyed," says Billie. "We actors are all gamblers but we risk things more important than money. We risk ourselves."

H.B. STUDIO

The door to 120 Bank Street in Greenwich Village is open to both established and aspiring artists pursuing a working home. Here they can develop their individual talents in an atmosphere of creative freedom. Serious students, of any age and any level of skill development, can receive instruction from a faculty of distinguished performing artists dedicated to passing on their experience. Classes are offered in many aspects of theater arts, including acting technique, scene study, script analysis, musical theater, speech, voice, scriptwriting, and directing. Low fees make it easier for the struggling artist to perfect his skills. Students are expected to join in the cooperative spirit of the school, most evident during the annual spring clean-up, when everyone pitches in to spruce up the H.B. home.

H.B. Studio was founded in 1945 by Herbert Berghof, whose guiding spirit keeps the light of hope for an American theater of service to its community kindled. Uta Hagen Berghof continues to direct the school in pursuit of this ideal and to pass on the fruits of her outstanding career as a great American actress to her privileged students.

Herbert Berghof Studio
120 Bank Street
New York, NY 10014
(212) 675-2370

ROUNDABOUT THEATER TOURS

The Roundabout Theater Company offers theater tours to London every fall and "exotic" tours to such places as India, Russia, and Bali in the spring. In London, you can see not only the best of London's productions and participate in discussions with directors, playwrights, actors, and critics, but you can also tour backstage, shop, and sightsee. The "exotic" trips include performances and visits to cultural sights and points of interest.

Roundabout Theater Company
100 East 17th Street
New York, NY 10003
(212) 420-1360

BOOKS

A Challenge for the Actor, by Uta Hagen (New York: Scribner's, 1991), is a revised and updated version of Uta Hagen's acclaimed acting text, *Respect for Acting*. The book is a synthesis of the knowledge and technique Miss Hagen developed over a lifetime of acting and teaching. Actors will learn how to find the characters they play within themselves and how to ground themselves in a reality that results in human behavior. Through a series of exercises that break down various acting problems, actors are able to practice and develop their technique in much the same way musicians play scales and dancers work out at the bar. The essential elements necessary for dramatic action are defined and methods for evoking true behavior are explained.

Three One-Act Plays about the Elderly, by Elyse Nass (New York: Samuel French, 1990), is a trilogy of one-act comedy dramas by award-winning playwright Elyse Nass that focus on the lives of older people. "Second Chance" is about a sixty-eight-year-old widow who decides to take up acting as a hobby and her neighbor's efforts to dissuade her. It was originally produced by the Quaigh Theater in New York City and by the San Diego Repertory Theater in California. "Admit One," about a seventy-five-year-old man who places an ad in the personals to find a wife, was presented at the Actors Studio in New York and the Barn Players' Senior Acting Program in Overland Park, Kansas. "Cat Connection" deals with two women in their sixties who meet accidentally on a park bench awaiting the arrival of a stray cat. It was presented at the Cubiculo Theater in New York City. It has also been presented by the Cultural Environ's Drama Workshop of Older Adults in New York and toured many senior centers. Production rights are available through Samuel French.

Samuel French, Inc.
46 West 25th Street
New York, NY 10010
(212) 206-8990

7623 Sunset Boulevard
Hollywood, CA 90046
(213) 876-0570

LITERATURE

The written word can communicate ideas and feelings; pass on knowledge; delve into the thoughts and experiences of others or come to terms with our own; explore different places and times; and provide hours of pleasure. The wealth of available literature would take lifetimes to consume. To contribute, all you need is pencil, paper, and dedication. Some of the greatest literature was written by people mature in years.

Goethe was eighty when he completed *Faust*. Oliver Wendell Holmes wrote some of his best work in his seventies.

You needn't produce great works of literature to reap the benefits of writing. Compiling your memoirs or writing about historic events you experienced would be a welcome gift to family members, future generations, and historians.

READING

Reading is rated by retirees as their number-one choice of leisure activities. Our vast system of public libraries makes an abundance of reading material available. Libraries provide discussion groups, classes, meet-the-author sessions, poetry readings, and many other kinds of programs. Book clubs bring the newest and best to your door, and specialty stores and dealers can find resources on almost any subject. Low vision or total blindness should not deter you: large print, braille, and talking books are easily accessible.

Strand Bookstore

The Strand Bookstore is the largest second-hand bookstore in the country. It contains more than two million used, out-of-print, and rare books. It also stocks review copies and remainder supplies of new books. Prices are low and the knowledgeable staff can help you locate whatever topic you are looking for. Mail-order service to anywhere in the world puts the Strand in close proximity to anyone in search of reading material at discount prices. A partial listing of titles is available or you may call for information.

Strand Bookstore
828 Broadway
New York, NY 10003
(212) 473-1452

Large Print

Some loss of vision is almost inevitable with aging. Half of all people over sixty-five have some noticeable loss of vision. Besides a good set of properly fitting eyeglasses, there are several things you can do to make reading more comfortable. Be sure you are in good light, and hold your head at a comfortable angle. A large, movable, floor-mounted magnifying lens will enlarge type. A small folding lens that can fit in your pocket or purse will do the trick when you're not at home. Many books and periodicals, such as the *Reader's Digest* and the *New York Times*, are available in large-type editions. Your library probably has a large print section.

Doubleday Large Print Home Library

Members of the Doubleday Large Print Home Library can select from a large collection of fiction and nonfiction books, including bestsellers, craft books, and crossword-puzzle and mystery books.

Doubleday Large Print Home Library
6550 East 30th Street
PO Box 6352
Indianapolis, IN 46206-6352
(317) 541-8920

Talking Books

Anyone who cannot hold, handle, or see a book well enough to read conventional print materials due to a visual or physical disability is eligible for materials from the National Library Service for the Blind and Physically Handicapped of the Library of Congress. The service maintains an extensive collection of recordings, including technical as well as recreational material, reaching more than five hundred thousand adults. For information, consult your local library, or contact:

National Library Service for the Blind
  and Physically Handicapped
Library of Congress
Washington, DC 20542
(202) 707-5100

WRITING

If you ever dreamed of writing, retirement is the perfect opportunity to realize your ambitions. Many resources exist to help you along. Classes, workshops, books, magazines, and computer software exist to help you sharpen your skills.

Books

The Elements of Style, by William Strunk, Jr., and E. B. White (New York: Macmillan, 1972), was written by a professor of English at Cornell University and was revised by his former student, E. B. White. True to its watchword, "omit needless words," it provides expert advice on the craft of writing in seventy-eight pages. Its humor, wisdom, and guiding principles make it an invaluable companion to any writer.

The Writers' Handbook, edited by Sylvia Burak (Boston: The Writer, updated annually), is a guide to what to write, how to write, and where to sell your writing is updated every year. It contains a comprehensive listing of markets including magazine, book, and theatrical publishers, and is complete with names, addresses, and editorial requirements. Leading authors contribute advice on the craft of writing. The guide is available in bookstores or directly from the publisher.

The Writer, Inc.
120 Boylston Street
Boston, MA 20116
(617) 423-3157

Magazines

Writing magazines are an excellent source of information on markets, techniques, books, contests, and conferences. They will keep you up-to-date on what's going on in publishing and supply you with ideas on how and what to write. Libraries and magazine stores carry a selection of such magazines. The following two are favorites of many writers.

The Writer
120 Boylston Street
Boston, MA 02116
(617) 423-3157

Writers' Digest
PO Box 2124
Harlan, IA 51593-2313

Writers' Conferences

Writers' conferences are excellent opportunities to increase your knowledge of writing and marketing techniques, to make contacts, and to share your work with others. Hundreds of conferences are held around the country. Some focus on a specific type of writing—scriptwriting, nonfiction, or fiction, for example. Others concentrate on a specific genre—mysteries, romance novels, or children's books. Many feature big-name guest speakers. Experienced writers provide instruction and social events give you a chance to mingle with agents, editors, and writers. Upcoming conferences are advertised in writing magazines such as *Writers' Digest*, which publishes a conference list each year. Shaw Guides also publishes a listing of conferences, including information on activities, facilities, and costs.

Shaw Guides, Inc.
625 Biltmore Way
Coral Gables, FL 33134
(305) 446-8888

Senior Scribes

James E. Kurtz, a retired journalist, marketer, and editor, organized a network of senior writers to keep in touch with one another called Senior Scribes. There are no membership dues, and Senior Scribes provides market information and other helpful data to encourage senior writers to continue writing.

Senior Scribes
c/o Poverty Press
PO Box 2035
Cape May, NJ 08204

Memories

Memories is a computer-software program designed to help you write an autobiography. It asks questions about the main events in your life and helps you compile your wisdom and experience into a document that can be passed on to future generations. The finished product is a printed book, complete with title page, dedication, and chapter headings. It is not necessary to be a computer wiz to use this tool. The manual is easily understandable and the program itself guides you through the process.

Memories
Senior Software Systems
8804 Wildridge Drive
Austin, TX 78759
(800) 637-9949

MUSIC

Like a good friend, music is always there for us. It lulls us to sleep as infants, bonds us to others in our youth, and enlivens us in our old age. It can take us back to another time, cheer us when we are sad, make us want to dance, and bring a tear to our eyes. Though there are few Mozarts, everyone makes music. We all sing in the shower or the car, hum along to our favorite tunes, or tap out a rhythm on our knees. If we feel like listening, all we need to do is turn on the radio, put on a record, or take out our instrument.

Retirement provides even more opportunities to enjoy music. There are always concerts to attend in parks, high schools, or symphony halls. Many are free and discounts for older people are often available. You can take advantage of your ability to attend at off hours and sit in on final rehearsals, which many orchestras and opera companies permit. It's also a great time to take up an instrument or go back to the one you played as a kid. You could join a choral group or sing in the church choir. If you can't find a group to join, start one of your own.

LEARN TO PLAY A MUSICAL INSTRUMENT

According to the American Music Conference, you are never too old to learn to play music. Research by Dr. Edwin Gordon of Temple University indicates that if you love to listen to music and can feel the beat, you can learn to play an instrument at any age. Because it is an activity you have freely chosen, you have even a better chance to succeed at it than very talented children whose parents *make* them play. The American Music Conference is so certain of your ability to play that they will send you a booklet entitled, "Yes You Can!" free of charge. Put your request in writing and send a self-addressed, stamped number 10 envelope to:

American Music Conference
Suite 1214
303 East Wacker Dr.
Chicago, IL 60601
(312) 856-8888

Related publications are available from the following sources.

"Choosing a Music Teacher" and *Directory of Nationally Certified Music Teachers*
The Music Teachers National Association
Department C, Suite 1432
617 Vine Street
Cincinnati, OH 45202–2434
(513) 421-1420

"So You've Always Wanted to Play the Piano?" and "The Possible Dream"
The National Piano Foundation
Suite 105, Department A

4020 McEwen
Dallas, TX 75244–5019
(214) 233-9107

AMATEUR CHAMBER MUSIC PLAYERS (ACMP)

If you love to play or sing chamber music, the Amateur Chamber Music Players can connect you with other players all across the United States and in fifty other countries. The ACMP is a voluntary, nonprofit association whose purpose is to facilitate the playing and singing of chamber music by enabling enthusiastic amateurs (and professionals who also play or sing for the love of it), to meet each other. Members are listed in and receive directories listing names, addresses, and phone numbers of chamber music players, noting the instrument they play and their proficiency level. If you're looking for others in your community to make music with, moving to a new community, or just passing through, you may contact the members listed in the directory and arrange to meet. One retired doctor and his wife travel around the country in their trailer complete with music chair and stands, finding music wherever they go.

Membership entitles you to an annual newsletter filled with information, articles, and anecdotes of interest to musicians. The ACMP also publishes a list of recommended chamber music, a list of books about chamber music, and maintains a music lending library at Hartford, Connecticut. Members can borrow music and books from this collection through the interlibrary loan system.

Amateur Chamber Music Players, Inc.
545 Eighth Avenue
New York, NY 10018
(212) 244-2778

COLLECTOR'S RECORD CLUB

Jazz enthusiasts can receive discounts on recordings and compact discs as well as a subscription to *Jazz Beat*, a magazine devoted to the appreciation of great jazz music.

GHB Jazz Foundation
Collector's Record Club
1206 Decatur Street
New Orleans, LA 70116
(504) 525-1776

SONG WRITING

Theresa Kosydar Rosecrants, a retired resident of Chicago, always wanted to put stories to music. But it wasn't until her family had grown and she retired from her job as assistant foreman at the Switchcraft Company that she was able to make her dream a reality. Drawing heavily from her childhood, she writes of growing up as a miner's daughter. One song tells of a poor family whose children wish that Santa would bring Mama some red roses and a guitar for Christmas. Her songs have been recorded by Hollywood Sessions and Country Creations.

The National Academy of Songwriters can provide you with information on writing and marketing songs. They can keep you up-to-date on workshops, conferences, books, and demos. They also publish a newspaper called *Song Talk* filled with interviews of the world's leading songwriters. For membership information, contact:

National Academy of Songwriters
Suite 780
6381 Hollywood Boulevard
Hollywood, CA 90029
(213) 463-7178

Bagaduce Music Lending Library

This library contains a large variety of music for piano, chamber ensemble, sacred and secular choral music with orchestral accompaniment, and popular vocal music. For a small yearly membership fee, you may keep borrowed music up to two months. Catalogues of available music will be sent upon request.

Bagaduce Library
Green's Hill
Blue Hill, ME 04614
(207) 374-5454

Workshops, Festivals, and Special Events

One of the best ways to learn new music, meet fellow musicians, and play with others is to attend one of the many workshops and special events across the country. Every February, Music for the Love of It publishes a directory of summer workshops in the US.

Music for the Love of It
67 Parkside Drive
Berkeley, CA 94705–2409
(415) 652-0551

For a directory of summer chamber music festivals and workshops, contact:

Chamber Music America, Inc.
545 Eighth Avenue,
New York, NY 10018
(212) 244-2772

Folk and country music are performed and celebrated by the following organizations; the first is discussed more fully in the Dance section and the second in the Arts and Crafts section.

Country Dance and Song Society
17 New South Street
Northampton, MA 01060
(413) 584-9913

Augusta Heritage Center
Davis and Elkins College
Elkins, WV 26241–3996
(304) 636-1903

BOOKS AND OTHER PUBLICATIONS

Reference books and music periodicals are published for all aspects of music, including specific types of music and instruments. Your local library may have a copy of *Music and Dance Periodicals* by Doris Robinson (Voorheesville, NY: Peri Press, 1990). This directory will help you locate those periodicals that pertain to your area of interest.

The National Square Dance Directory provides information on records, callers, and other aspects of square-dance music. Order a copy from:

National Square Dance Directory
P.O. Box 54055
Jackson, MS 39288
(800) 542-4010

Music for the Love of It is a newsletter for recreational musicians containing articles on technique, musical interpretation, compositions, and workshops.

Music for the Love of it
Suite 2, Box 75
2980 College Avenue
Berkeley, CA 94705
(415) 654-9134

The Musical Mainstream is devoted to the needs of blind and visually impaired musicians. Articles are available in large print, braille, and flexible-disc formats. Subscriptions are free to eligible blind and handicapped persons.

Library of Congress
National Library Service for the Blind and Physically
    Handicapped
1292 Taylor Street NW
Washington, DC 20542
(202) 707-5100

CRAFTS

People have a special reverence for the work they produce by hand. The ability to use tools, construct dwellings, weave fibers into cloth, and cook food places us above the ape. The cave drawings of early man testify to our drive to translate our experiences into visual representations and our need to adorn our environment. We take pride in our skill, mastery, and accomplishments. Through the medium of wood, clay, glass, stone, paint, and fabric, we express our creativity and individuality. Frustrations are released when we pound and shape. Concentrating on the task before us, all other distractions are shut out. We are unaware of outside cares or the passage of time. The endless objects produced provide tangible rewards for our efforts, resulting in things we can see, touch, and use.

The satisfactions derived from working with our hands can be gained from countless crafts involving beads, ceramics, jewelry, leather, models, stained glass, fibers, and wood. The visual arts, including painting, drawing, sculpture, photography, and film offer many outlets for creativity. For any art or craft you choose, you will find instruction, supplies, and others who share your interest. There are also opportunities to exhibit and sell your work. Some people turn their hobbies into second careers or return to their artistic pursuits after retirement.

At the age of sixty, Jeanette Gottlieb of Lawrence, New York, turned her hobby into a full-time commitment. Bunka, a way of painting with stitchery, has become her obsession. Her home is like a museum of bunka art. She makes frequent television appearances as an expert in this unusual craft and arranges exhibits of her work. She also teaches adult education classes in bunka painting.

Jackson Lee Nesbit was highly regarded as a regional artist in the South during the late 1930s and 1940s, but financial problems forced him to abandon his etching and printmaking and turn to business. He opened his own company selling calendars, key chains, and promotional items imprinted with advertising messages. When he sold his company in 1987, he was able to return to the career he abandoned more than twenty years earlier (*AARP Bulletin*, Spring 1991).

"It occurred to me that we would have enough money to live on from the sale of the business, even if I never sold another print." His work, which focuses on rural themes, has initiated a revival of interest and is featured in museums and galleries across the country. He is delighted to be able to pursue his art free from financial pressure and to see that his creations are still attracting attention.

Though fine, detailed work may become more difficult with age, there are many simple adaptations that can increase your enjoyment. If arthritis has weakened your hands, use electric scissors. If your hands are shaky, pin down your material. If your vision is less than perfect, always work in a well lit area. (That goes for everyone.) A floor-mounted magnifier or one worn around your neck will also be helpful. Choose patterns with large areas of color and minimal detail. Use bright colors, thicker yarn, and large-eye needles. Instead of needlepoint canvas, use rug canvas. Instead of size 2 knitting needles, use size 12. Learn to rely more on your sense of touch. Many blind people are expert knitters. The textural designs they create bring a new dimension to the craft.

AMERICAN CRAFT COUNCIL

The American Craft Council, a national, nonprofit educational organization serving more than 35,000 members, works to encourage craftsmen and to foster public appreciation of their work. It maintains a resource library with information on books, periodicals, videos, schools, festivals, and individual artists. It has established the American Crafts Museum in New York City, where the finest examples of American crafts are exhibited. It also publishes *American Crafts* magazine, which profiles crafts and craft people, surveys trends, and presents up-to-date listings of craft events.

American Craft Council
72 Spring Street
New York, NY 10012
(212) 247-0630

THE ELDER CRAFTSMEN SHOP

Situated on Manhattan's fashionable Upper East Side is a unique store that sells only items made by craftsmen over the age of fifty-five. Here you will find handcrafted quilts, sweaters, toys, clothing, rugs, Christmas ornaments, and all manner of folk arts made by talented craftsmen from all over the US. The Elder Craftsmen Shop is a nonprofit organization that lets older craftsmen choose whether to sell their work on a consignment basis or to receive payment for piece work done at home. It was founded in 1955 to educate and advise older people in the making and selling of fine handcrafts; it also offers how-to information on marketing and setting up one's own Elder Craftsmen Shop. Those interested in becoming an Elder Craftsman may submit their work for review by mail or in person. There are similar shops and cooperatives across the country. Contact the New York Elder Craftsmen for their locations and further information.

The Elder Craftsmen Shop
851 Lexington Avenue
New York, NY 10021
(212) 861-5260

ARTS AND CRAFTS WORKSHOPS

Beginners and experts alike can immerse themselves in stimulating and pleasant surroundings; learn from renowned teachers; gain hands-on experience; enhance their artistic and technical skills; and enjoy the company of fellow artists at creative retreats across the country. The following is a listing of some established arts and crafts workshops.

Penland

Penland occupies 470 acres in the Blue Ridge Mountains of Western North Carolina. In this isolated, rural environment, students of all ability levels receive instruction from practicing studio craftsmen in such arts as bookmaking, ceramics, drawing, fiber arts, glassmaking, metalwork, papermaking, photography, printmaking, and woodwork. Well equipped studios are open for use twenty-four hours a day. Other facilities include a library, exhibition space, and sales gallery. The surrounding acres provide trails for hiking and recreational activities. Accommodations are rustic but include excellent meals. Sessions are held in spring, summer, and fall.

Penland School
Penland, NC 28765–0037
(704) 765-2359

Haystack Mountain School of Crafts

Located on Deer Isle, off the rugged coast of Maine, this internationally respected crafts center provides an idyllic setting for the pursuit of artistic excellence. Designed by Edward Larrabee Barnes, the campus consists of small, shingled buildings nestled among trees that are perfectly suited to their environment and purpose. Enrollment is limited to provide a balance between departments, ages, and ability levels. Studios are open twenty-four hours a day, and evening programs feature slide presentations and lectures. Workshops include blacksmithing, basketry, graphics, book arts, and quilting, and work with such materials as clay, metals, fibers, paper, wood, and glass. In addition to summer programs, Haystack sponsors short-term conferences and workshops in May, September, and October.

Haystack Mountain School of Crafts
Deer Isle, ME 04627–0087
(207) 348-2306

Oregon School of Arts and Crafts

The Oregon School of Arts and Crafts, located ten minutes from downtown Portland, occupies 8 acres of fruit orchards. Its facilities are a blend of beauty and function. The studios are flanked by large windows offering natural light and spectacular views of the coastal ridge. The library has a collection of more than three thousand books. Works of regional and national artists are exhibited in the gallery, and delicious, affordable meals are served in the cafeteria. During the summer months, week-long sessions are taught by nationally known artists in such arts as acrylic painting, drawing, Japanese papermaking, machine embroidery, landscape photography, calligraphy, and ceramics. Though there is no on-campus housing, accommodations can be arranged with nearby residents.

Oregon School of Arts and Crafts
8245 SW Barnes Road
Portland, OR 97225
(503) 297-5544

Arrowmont School of Arts and Crafts

Arrowmont sits on a 70-acre wooded hillside three miles from the entrance to the Great Smoky Mountains National Park in eastern Tennessee. One- or two-week sessions in such arts and crafts as weaving, basketry, quilting, enameling, pottery, tapestry, and painting are taught by prominent artists. Within the complex are well equipped studios, a supply store, a library, and a gallery. Simply furnished cottages provide on-campus housing. Slide presentations, lectures, musical performances, and demonstrations round out the week's activities.

Arrowmont School of Arts and Crafts
PO Box 567
Gatlinburg, TN 37738
(615) 436-5860

Horizons

The Horizons Art Center is nestled amid 50 acres of woodland and pasture in the scenic foothills of the Berkshires. Art enthusiasts from coast to coast take advantage of Horizons weekend and week-long workshops in subjects such as painting, drawing, fiber arts, metalwork, woodwork, ceramics, photography, and glass blowing. Horizons also runs two international intensives in Mexico and England focusing on such media as jewelry, stained glass, and ceramics.

Horizons
374 Old Montague Road
Amherst, MA 01002
(413) 594-4841

Anderson Ranch Arts Center

The Anderson Ranch Arts Center is located in Snowmass Village, a cosmopolitan mountain resort ten miles west of Aspen. The 14,000-foot peaks of the Colorado Rockies provide an ideal setting for these three-week-long workshops. Once a sheep farm, the property contains historic log barns and a ranch house. Accomplished artists and committed students receive intensive hands-on experience in ceramics, painting, photography, and woodworking. Students are housed on campus, and meals are served in the cafeteria. The Aspen/ Snowmass area has many cultural attractions, including the Aspen Music Festival, Dance Aspen, the Aspen Art Museum, the International Design Conference, and the Aspen Repertory Theater.

Anderson Arts Ranch
PO Box 5598
Snowmass Village, CO 81615
(303) 923-3181

Augusta Heritage Center

Celebrate the folk arts at the Augusta Heritage Center. Here traditional dance, crafts, music, and storytelling flourish. You can study the hammered dulcimer, Cajun dance, quiltmaking, storytelling, whittling, old-time fiddling, dance calling, and clogging. The annual Augusta festival features music, song, dance, stories, food, and crafts from the hills of Appalachia and the Old West. The mountains of central West Virginia, on the edge of the Monongahela National Forest, offer opportunities for white-water rafting, canoeing, caving, rock climbing, backpacking, and swimming.

Augusta Heritage Center
Davis and Elkins College
Elkins, WV 26241–3996
(304) 636-1903

BOOKS AND OTHER PUBLICATIONS

The Crafts Supply Sourcebook, by Margaret A. Boyd (Crozet, VA: Betterway Publications), is a comprehensive shop-by-mail guide that will tell you where to find supplies, tools, equipment, organizations, and publications for all sorts of crafts. It contains more than 2,500 detailed listings, including address, phone numbers, and a summary of each source. The book can be purchased in bookstores or ordered from the publisher.

Betterway Publications
PO Box 219
Crozet, VA 22932
(804) 823-5661

These publishers maintain a large selection of books on various arts and crafts. Look for them in your local bookstore or write to the publishers for catalogues.

Storey's Books for Country Living
Storey Communications, Inc.
Schoolhouse Road
Pownal, VT 05261
(800) 827-8673

Chilton Book Company
One Chilton Way
Rador, PA 19089
(800) 345-1214

The biennial *American Art Directory* lists art schools in the US and around the world. It also includes information on scholarships, fellowships, art organizations, and associations as well as periodicals. Look for this book in your library or order a copy from the publisher.

Jaques Cattell Press
R. R. Bowker Company
245 West 17th Street
New York, NY 10011
(212) 337-6934

Magazines and newsletters are excellent resources for keeping up-to-date with information on craft shops, fairs, galleries, supplies, techniques, and workshops. The American Craft Council, which publishes *American Craft*, can provide you with a listing of such publications. Some of the magazines available are described below.

Crafting Today provides instructions and patterns for a variety of crafts, including needle crafts, woodworking, and doll making. Special columns focus on gift wrapping, new products, and different ways to use favorite craft materials.

Crafting Today
PO Box 517
Mount Morris, IL 61054–7993

Each issue of *Crafts 'n Things* contains instructions and patterns for a wide variety of crafting projects, including holiday and seasonal items as well as resource information and regular columns.

Crafts 'n Things
14 Main Street
Park Ridge, IL 60068

The Crafts Fair Guide is an up-to-date listing of crafts fairs across the country, published four times a year.

The Crafts Fair Guide
PO Box 5062
Mill Valley, CA 94962
(415) 332-5499

American Artist magazine, devoted to the visual arts, contains articles on tools, techniques, competitions, festivals, galleries, and individual artists.

American Artist
1 Color Court
Marion, OH 43306
(800) 347-6969

≈

CHAPTER VII

Sports and Fitness

≋

"Once you're over the hill,
you pick up speed."
MOTTO OF THE OVER THE HILL GANG

"Exercise is the closest thing we have to an anti-aging pill," says Dr. Alexander Leaf of the Harvard Medical School. There is plenty of evidence to support his claim. Research shows that many of the problems once attributed to aging such as slowing down, declining muscle strength, and fatigue are actually the result of a sedentary lifestyle. Eighty percent of the health problems once associated with aging are now thought to be preventable or postponable if a person keeps fit.

Exercise strengthens the heart and lungs, increases circulation, reduces body fat, relieves stress, keeps bones strong, and lowers blood pressure. It strengthens and tones your muscles and keeps joints, tendons, and ligaments flexible, allowing you to move more easily. It increases your energy level, aids digestion, helps you sleep better, improves your appearance and overall sense of well-being. Following an exercise program gives you a sense of self-reliance, self-mastery, power, control, and an opportunity to set and achieve goals. You don't have to

208

be a marathon runner to achieve results. A study conducted by the Institute for Aerobics Research and the Cooper Clinic in Dallas shows that moderate exercise can substantially reduce your chance of dying of heart disease or cancer.

It doesn't matter when you start. You can reap the benefits of exercise at any age. Those who show the biggest health gains are those who are the most sedentary. In his book, *Fitness After 50*, (New York, NY: Scribner, 1969), Dr. Herbert DeVries, retired director of the Andrus Gerontology Center, states, "Men and women of sixty and seventy become as fit and energetic as those twenty to thirty years younger. The ones who improved the most were the ones who had been the least active and most out of shape."

Sustained, strenuous exercise is no longer considered the only way to reach fitness. Experts now believe that the equivalent of a few brisk walks a week is all you need to improve your odds of living a long and healthy life. Studies show that activities of any kind, including useful activities such as cleaning the house, mowing the lawn, or taking out the garbage enhance longevity. Trimming the hedge burns more calories than weight training, and shoveling snow burns more than jumping rope.

Staying fit need not be a chore. It can be a great deal of fun. The secret is to pick an activity you enjoy. If you like doing it, you'll be more likely to keep it up. The pleasure it provides will enhance the benefits by improving your mental state and stamina. Set aside a particular time of day when you feel most like exercising and stick with it. You'll want your exercise routine to become a habit you'll miss if you don't.

Most people can exercise safely without fear of health risks if they begin gradually. It is advisable to consult a doctor before starting any exercise routine, especially if you are over sixty and have a disease or disability, or if you are taking medication.

Go slowly at first. It takes time to develop muscle strength, endurance, and flexibility. Pushing your body too far too soon only causes injury. Start with short five- to ten-minute sessions a few times a week. Gradually increase to fifteen- or thirty-minutes, three to four times a week.

Listen to your body. If it hurts, it's time to stop. Exercise should leave you invigorated or pleasantly fatigued. If you feel totally depleted, you've done too much. After vigorous exercise, your heart rate will quicken, you'll breathe heavier, and you may experience mild sweating and muscle soreness. These are all normal reactions. However, if you should experience any unusual symptoms, such as shortness of breath, chest discomfort, blueness in lips or fingers, dizziness, or nausea, stop exercising and consult your doctor.

Warming up before starting and cooling down at the end of your routine prevent injuries. Your warm-up can consist of five to ten minutes of light calisthenics, jogging in place, or walking briskly to get your circulation going. Include some stretching exercises in your routine. Stretching improves flexibility, which enhances your performance of daily tasks, such as raking the leaves or improving your tennis or golf swing. At the end of your session, allow a few minutes to cool down so your muscles can recuperate gradually. You can cool down by doing the same activity at a slower pace.

There are many activities that can help keep you fit as well as add pleasure to your life. They can also bring you in contact with others who share your interests. For instance, bowling in a league is lots of fun, and though it may not be all the exercise you need to stay fit, it encourages you to keep your muscles toned and stretched so you can perform your best for your team. Because your sessions are on a regular schedule and people are counting on you to show up, you're not apt to skip a session even if you're feeling a little tired or blue that day. John Venturello's teammates count on him to keep up his average and, though he is the oldest bowler on the team, he doesn't disappoint them. At one hundred years old, he's still bowling strikes.

Your community probably offers many kinds of fitness activities. It is not necessary to join a private health club or country club to find sports facilities. Parks and recreation departments operate tennis courts, golf courses, bicycle paths, swimming pools, and skating rinks. YMCAs offer many types of games and sports, including fitness and weight training. Your local bowling alley can hook you up with a league. Hospitals, senior centers, and high schools run fitness programs, such as "mall walking" groups and baseball leagues. Fancy equipment and organized activities aren't the only way to keep fit. It can be as simple as going out for a walk.

WALKING

Walking is the most popular form of exercise among older adults. It is considered one of the best overall exercises because it improves circulation, strengthens leg muscles, and can provide a good cardiovascular workout without a lot of wear and tear on the body. Though it may seem tame in comparison to other sports, a brisk twenty- to thirty-minute walk three or four times a week is sufficient exercise to maintain health and is much less stressful on the big muscles, tendons, and joints than jogging, aerobic dancing, or racket sports.

There are many advantages to walking. Just about anyone can do it. You don't need to take lessons or concentrate on your technique. It is as natural as breathing. It requires no special equipment, can be done anywhere, any time, alone or with company, and is the safest form of exercise around. Best of all, it's pleasant.

You don't just feel good *after* a walk—you feel good *while* you're doing it. You can take your Walkman along and listen to music or just enjoy your surroundings. Because you don't have to concentrate on what you are doing, you can let your mind wander where it will or use the time to work out life's problems. Walking can put you in a state of mind where solutions to things that have eluded you just pop into your head. Albert Einstein came upon the theory of relativity while walking on a hillside.

Walking is often prescribed for people recovering from injury, illness, or chronic health problems and is effective in combating many health problems associated with aging. It can be effective in fighting the pain and stiffness of arthritis and can help build strength to carry out daily activities. It can help improve balance by reducing the incidence of injury due to falling; fight osteoporosis by strengthening bones; ward off heart disease; and speed up sluggish digestion.

Though it may take a little longer, walking can provide the same conditioning results as more strenuous activities. The fitness benefits of walking can be enhanced by increasing speed, distance, adding weights, or walking up or down hills. Strolling at three miles per hour consumes 240 calories per hour. At a pace of five to ten miles per hour, walking burns 500 calories, matching the calorie-burning rate for jogging.

To get started on a walking program, decide what time of day you're the most free to enjoy exercising and schedule that in for your regular walk. You can walk anywhere: through parks, shopping malls, golf courses, cemeteries, or along waterfronts. Though you don't need any special clothing for walking, you might want to have a special outfit that puts you in the mood. Be sure it's comfortable and provides adequate protection from the weather. You might want to invest in a pair of walking shoes. Manufacturers have developed excellent athletic shoes just for walking.

Like any other exercise, start with a warm-up. It should include stretching exercises and five to ten minutes of walking at an easy pace. Walk comfortably and naturally and allow your arms to hang loosely. They will automatically swing in opposition to your feet. Let your heels strike the ground and transfer your weight to your toes. Keep your spine straight and your head high but don't force any walking posture. Just do what comes naturally. Start by walking as far as you can with ease and gradually increase your pace or distance. At the end of your walk, cool off by decreasing your pace.

That's all there is to it, though you can take it further if you want. Speed walking is increasing in popularity and converting many one-time joggers to its ranks. Speed walking has its own technique, characterized by a strange waddle. Comical though it may appear to the uninitiated, this form allows walkers to reach high speeds and provides an excellent aerobic workout. You can also enter walking competitions and join walking clubs where you can enjoy the company of other walkers.

BOOKS AND OTHER PUBLICATIONS

Your public library or bookstore will have many books on walking. The following is one that you may find useful.

Walking for Exercise and Pleasure is available free from:

President's Council on Physical Fitness and Sports
450 5th Street NW
Suite 7103
Washington, DC 20001
(202) 272-3430

BICYCLING

Bicycling isn't only good for you; it's a lot of fun. It can be an excellent way to stay fit, a useful means of transportation, and a wonderful way to travel. It is a popular sport for people over fifty, many of whom bicycled as children. Ed Delano of Davis, California, hadn't cycled for thirty-nine years when, at age fifty-eight, he returned to the sport. He now competes annually in US Cycling Federation competitions, usually winning top honors in his class. He made four solo cross-country trips, including one to his fiftieth class reunion. Ed, or Foxy Grandpa as he is called, is now eighty-five. "I'm slowing down," he says, "but I'm still in better shape than the average sixty-year-old."

Experts agree on the value of bicycling as a fitness sport. Like running, it tones the large muscles of the lower body and stimulates the cardiovascular system, but is easier on the joints. Dr. Kenneth H. Cooper, author of *The Aerobic Program for Total Well-Being* (New York, NY: M. Evans, 1982), considers cycling, "a good match for running and swimming. The training effects on the internal organs are identical in those three sports."

Bike touring is a marvelous way to travel. The experience of cycling on quiet, scenic routes through small towns and villages while enjoying the open air is unparalleled. Guidebooks and maps are available, detailing points of interest and places to stay. Many organizations run group cycling tours all over the world for people of varying ability levels. It is not necessary to be a trained athlete to enjoy touring. Leonard Bauer, fifty-four, from Galveston, Texas, signed up for a tour through the Dutch countryside. "I hadn't been on a bike in thirty years. My thigh muscles were a bit sore the first few days, but it felt great to get the exercise. And it's true what they say—you never forget how to ride a bike."

Tandem bicycling is becoming very popular again. Riding tandem solves the problem of disparity between the athletic abilities of spouses, friends, or family members. Both can ride together and get to the same place at the same time. It's ideal for touring, and competitively it is one of the most exciting matches every year at the world cycling championships. For information on tandem bicycling, contact:

Tandem Club of America
c/o Jack Goertz
2220 Vanessa Drive
Birmingham, AL 35242
(205) 991-5519

The proper equipment, clothing, and technique can make cycling a safe and comfortable sport. Bikecentennial, the largest cycling organization in the nation, makes the following suggestions:

• Wear a helmet. Today's bicycle helmets are lightweight and effective. The protection they give to your head outweighs any cost and inconvenience. Consider it a necessity.
• Choose comfortable clothing of lightweight, breathable fabric in bright colors. You'll want to be visible on the road. Special cycling shorts are now available that won't bunch up or cut off circulation in your thighs, but any shorts that allow free leg movement and are long enough to prevent the skin inside your thighs from rubbing against the saddle will do. Most athletic shoes will do for starters. If you plan to tour for several days, you might want to invest in a pair of special stiff-soled cycling shoes specifically made for biking.
• Obey all the rules of the road. Most states treat bicycles as a vehicle, meaning all traffic regulations apply. Stop at stop signs and traffic signals. Know and use the proper hand signals for left and right turns. When riding in city traffic, pay special attention to your surroundings. Watch for storm-sewer grates that can grab a wheel, car doors opening in your path, potholes that can unseat you, and pedestrians who are watching for cars but not for bicycles. Ride with a defensive attitude. Assume the motorist or pedestrian doesn't see you, even if he or she is looking right at you.

The secret to efficient, comfortable cycling is in the proper use of gears. Shifting gears is simple. Don't be afraid to use all the gears available to you. Low gear will help you climb a hill without tiring as quickly. High gear will help when you're going down hills or backed by a powerful tail wind. Get to know your particular bike, so you can make use of all it was meant to do.

With all the choices available, buying a bike can be a dizzying experience. Shopping at a reputable dealer will save you a lot of problems. His knowledge and experience can help you choose the proper bike. They have a vested interest in your satisfaction, because they count on your return business for accessories and repairs. Make sure your dealer is a member of the National Bicycle Dealers Association.

Do some homework before shopping. Know what type of riding you plan to do. Your bike should be suited to your riding interest. You don't want to end up with too much or too little, or the wrong type of bicycle. Consider how often or how far you'll ride, and what type of roads you'll be traveling. Do you want to go fast and light or will you be carrying a load for camping tours? The better you can define your interests, the more your supplier can guide you to the right choice.

Bikecentennial can provide you with more detailed information. A free catalogue listing books on equipment, maintenance, fitness, where to go cycling and more is available from them.

BIKECENTENNIAL

Bikecentennial is a cross-country bicycle route created in 1973 in observance of the US bicentennial. The TransAmerica Bicycle trail remains the backbone of its 17,000-mile National Bicycle Route Network. Today, Bikecentennial serves more than 20,000 members and 150 affiliated clubs nationwide. It produces and distributes a variety of bicycling safety and education materials, including *Bicycle Forum*, a quarterly magazine; *Cyclists' Yellow Pages*, a resource guide; and the *Cyclosource Catalog*, the largest collection of current cycling information available anywhere, including maps and touring guides. They also offer group tours and serve as an advocacy force representing the interests of cyclists at the national level.

Bikecentennial
PO Box 8308
Missoula, MT 59807
(406) 721-1776

LEAGUE OF AMERICAN WHEELMEN

The League of American Wheelmen is a nationwide association of bicyclists that protect cyclists' rights and promotes safe and effective cycling. More than 500 affiliated clubs bring cyclists together for rides and rallies. Members receive *Bicycle USA* magazine, which contains articles on the latest events, equipment, and leading personalities in the world of bicycling. The *Cycling Calendar*, published annually, lists over 500 different events. *Bicycle USA Almanac* contains information on clubs, events, books, magazines, organizations, and lobbyists. Bicycle USA Tourfinder will help you plan adventures worldwide.

League of American Wheelmen
Suite 209
6707 Whitestone Road
Baltimore, MD 21207-4106
(301) 944-3399

BICYCLE FEDERATION OF AMERICA

The Bicycle Federation of America was founded in 1977 to promote the safe use of bicycles. It serves as a clearinghouse for information on all aspects of bicycling and works as an advocate for bicyclists' interests.

Bicycle Federation of America
1818 R Street NW
Washington, DC 20009
(202) 332-6986

TENNIS

Tennis is an ideal lifetime sport. Regular participation improves your strength, endurance, energy level, weight, appearance, and general sense of well-being. It keeps you actively involved with people of different ages and social backgrounds as well as with your peers. You will enjoy the success of personal improvement as you reach for higher goals. It is both a competitive and cooperative game. You can share the joys of success in a team effort; be comforted by partners in the face of defeat; or savor the pleasure of successfully meeting a younger opponent's power and strength with your experience, technique, and strategy.

Ken Beer of Hillsborough, California, started playing tennis when he was a pilot for Pan Am. Now at eighty-seven, he holds fifty-three national senior titles, including number one player in the US National Tennis Association's "eighty-five and over" bracket. "I try to hit about a thousand balls a day," he says. "The only way a person stays alive at my age is to take a keen interest in something and be challenged. For me, that's tennis. It gets me outdoors and helps me meet good people. Frankly, a person without a challenge is on the downhill" (*New York Times*, January 28, 1991).

Proper equipment can enhance your enjoyment and performance as well as help avoid injury. It is important to use a racket that is the right size and weight and has proper string tension to prevent shoulder and elbow injury. Pay special attention to the fit of your socks and shoes, avoiding shoes that are worn down or lack support. Be sure to warm up and stretch your muscles before playing and cool down after a game.

THE UNITED STATES TENNIS ASSOCIATION

The United States Tennis Association recognizes the value and potential of the senior player and encourages senior tennis as a means of healthful recreation and fitness. The USTA Senior Tennis Council monitors thousands of seniors in tournament play every year, including the USTA Senior National Championships. It also promotes the USTA National Championships for Wheelchair Tennis. All players who earn national ranking receive certificates and have their names printed in the USTA Tennis Yearbook. Players earning the highest rankings are asked to represent the United States in national competition. Recreational players are supported by the USTA through two programs: USTA Senior Recreational Doubles and the USTA Senior Recreational Tennis League. The council publishes a monthly column, "Senior Scoop," in *Tennis USA*, the USTA's membership newspaper. The USTA also publishes a national directory of senior tennis programs, including a program synopsis, the number of participants, names of contact persons, and the name, address, and telephone number of the organizations.

United States Tennis Association
707 Alexander Road
Princeton, NJ 08540-6399
(609) 452-2580

SKIING

Skiing might not be the first sport that comes to mind when you think of older athletes, but is very popular among the over-fifty set. According to the National Ski Areas Association, there are more than 200,000 downhill skiers age fifty-five and over in America. That number increases to beyond a half-million when you add the cross-country participants. Many of these skiers started when they were in their teens or younger, but a surprising number did not begin skiing until after they retired. Florence Woo has been an avid skier for twenty years, though she didn't start until she was sixty-five years old. "I started everything after I was sixty-five," she says. "It wasn't hard. Once you want to do something you do it. It is persistence that counts. You just point your skis down the hill and you feel like you're floating (*The Vail Trails Pastimes*, February 26, 1988).

Many factors lure older adults to the slopes. New technology provides warmth, safety, and ease of movement the old equipment could not. Improvements in teaching methods and mountain grooming make the sport a lot more pleasant and easier to learn. Many ski-area operators encourage older skiers by providing discounts, special lessons, and sometimes free use of facilities. They feel that having older skiers on the slopes is good for business. They inspire younger skiers to stick with it. Older skiers themselves have done a lot to promote the sport among their age group by organizing clubs that provide camaraderie and encouragement.

The most difficult thing about downhill skiing is taking that first run. Pushing off into the unknown is scary for anyone. The secret to conquering the mountain is to focus on the task at hand rather than allowing your anxieties to overwhelm you. If you stand at the bottom of the mountain and look up, reaching the bottom in one piece may seem impossible. But you don't ski the whole mountain at once. You only ski a little piece at a time. If you concentrate on the terrain under your feet, you will confidently cover as much ground at a time as is comfortable and surprise yourself at your capabilities.

Downhill skiing provides continual challenges for every level of ability. Each time you reach a goal, you begin to see the next challenge. You start out wanting to learn to snowplow, then to make parallel turns. Next you'll want to ski the mountain from its summit, and someday you'll even try the black diamond slope named "Jaws of Death." Accomplishing your goal is a thrill, whatever the level. Successfully skiing the "bunny slope" for the first time is as exciting as winning the giant slalom. There is always another challenge to meet.

The safest way to learn downhill skiing is to take lessons. Don't let your friends take you to the top of the mountain and use the "sink or swim" method. Terror is not a good teacher. Almost every ski area has a ski school and many have special classes for older adults. Elderhostels across the country offer ski instruction for beginners and intermediates.

Get into shape before going to the slopes. Skiing can be exhausting. For beginners, just putting on your equipment can be an ordeal. It is also important to warm up before skiing and to wear protective clothing. Don't forget the sun screen and goggles. Your chances of injury are greatly reduced if you remain in control and don't take chances beyond your ability. You're at high risk for injury when you're tired. Stop skiing before you become overly fatigued.

Cross-country skiing is becoming very popular. It takes less time to learn, costs less, is safer, and is easier on the joints than downhill. It ranks among the highest aerobic activities and is considered by some even more beneficial than jogging. Cross-country skiing's gliding movement takes less effort and creates less jarring impact than jogging, yet because of the cold it burns more calories. Like swimming, cross-country skiing uses all the muscle groups and can be learned and enjoyed at any age. All members of the family can enjoy it together. It is a wonderful activity to do with your grandchildren. It's also a good way for singles to get to know others.

Another advantage of cross-country skiing is that you can ski practically anywhere as long as there is snow. Many downhill ski areas also have groomed trails for cross-country. There are resorts, trails, ranches, and lodges all over the country where you can ski. The Cross-Country Ski Areas Association puts out a guide called "The Best of Cross-Country Skiing," with listings of more than five hundred cross-country ski areas plus tips for beginners, coupons on lessons, rentals, and trail passes. To get a copy, contact:

Cross-Country Ski Areas Association
259 Bolton Road
Winchester, NH 03470
(603) 239-4341

OVER THE HILL GANG

The Over the Hill Gang was founded by three over-fifty ski instructors who suspected the reason they were the only gray heads on the mountain was not because older people lost the interest or capacity to ski but that they had no one to ski with. They were right. "The gang" has seen astonishing growth since its inception in 1977. It now has thousands of members in local clubs across the country and continues to grow at a rapid pace. The main purpose of the group is to promote camaraderie among active older adults who enjoy participating in sports with their peers. Though skiing is still the mainstay of the group, "gangsters" enjoy many other activities, such as sailing, surfing, bicycling, ballooning, tennis, and trips all over the world. Jack Floberg, a retired attorney, joined the group when his ski partner of forty years was grounded by his doctor. "I really love to ski, and have been doing it for fifty years. This club gives me a chance to ski with people who are my contemporaries, even if it's only for a day or two a week. I still get a big thrill standing on top of a hill, appreciating the view. It's the world the way God envisioned it," he says. Tom Gaylord, fifty-seven, says he joined because, "I used to ski with my kids, but they got too good for me and were tired of waiting at the bottom of the hill for me to finish a run" (*Vista USA*, Summer 1987).

If you would like to join "the gang," contact:

Over the Hill Gang
6635 South Dayton Street, #220
Englewood, CO 80111
(303) 790-2724

THE 70-PLUS SKI CLUB

If you're not seventy years old, the only way you can join the 70-Plus ski club is to have a spouse who is. It's no use lying about your age. If you think they won't check, you're wrong. They will. If you are lucky enough to meet this requirement, you are encouraged to share in the discounts, trips, and events members enjoy. More than 6,000 skiers worldwide belong. Lloyd Lambert, the clubs' founder, just turned ninety but is still a youngster compared to the club's oldest member, who is one hundred.

70-Plus Ski Club
104 East Side Drive
Ballston Lake, NY 12019
(518) 399-5458

Inner Skiing, by Timothy Gallwey and Bob Kriegel (New York: Bantam, 1979), teaches you to ski as naturally as your parents taught you to walk. The secret is in enjoying the process, experiencing the moment, and conquering the fears and doubts that interfere with your innate ability to perform well. Ask for the book in your local library or bookstore, or contact the publisher.

Bantam Books
666 Fifth Avenue
New York, NY 10020
(212) 765-6500

SWIMMING

Swimming is called the perfect sport because it exercises all the major muscles, toning and firming the whole body at once. It provides an excellent cardiovascular workout without straining the joints and with little chance of injury. It builds endurance, balance, strength, and flexibility and can be enjoyed throughout life. It is ideal for people who because of injury, arthritis, heart conditions, or chronic back problems are unable to participate in other activities. According to the President's Council on Physical Fitness and Sports, swimming has the most participants of any sport: 66.1 million Americans swim.

Water's unique properties make it an excellent medium for exercise. Buoyancy holds the body up, cushioning and supporting the muscles. In a horizontal position, weight-bearing stress is eliminated. The heart enlarges, pumping 10 to 20 percent more blood than usual with each contraction. You weigh one tenth as much in water as you do on land and can work harder and longer with less strain to the muscles. From a fitness standpoint, the biggest advantage of water is the resistance it provides. A half-hour of water exercise can produce the same results as two hours of land exercise, yet your motions seem effortless.

The therapeutic and health enhancing effect of water are all well and good, but many people are drawn to it for its sensual qualities. It feels good to be in the water. It's soothing and relaxing. It can provide privacy and quiet, a way to calm the mind as well as to strengthen the body. Diana Schuback, sixty-nine years old, swims between one-half and three-quarters of a mile four or five times a week. "As an artist, I need seclusion. Swimming is a way of removing myself from the tempo of life. It isolates me. Where else would you get that quiet? I don't want to go to the movies. I don't want to be entertained. I want to be suspended someplace in cool water. In the pool is where I start filtering and sifting out. It gives me clarity (*New York Times Magazine*, April 29, 1990).

Swimming can also be a social activity. You can join a team, swim club, or enter competitions. YMCAs and community centers offer a variety of swimming activities, including water exercise and sports. If you don't know how to swim or feel a bit rusty, you will find a Red Cross swim class in almost any community where you can learn in a comfortable, safe environment.

UNITED STATES MASTERS SWIMMING

Masters Swimming provides opportunities for adults to participate in organized swim activities ranging from lap swimming to international competitions. There are more than 25,000 members in 450 local clubs around the country. You can join a team or remain independent and still get the benefits of membership, which include health insurance and the USMS newsletter filled with articles of interest to swimmers. The US

Masters competitions draw enthusiastic crowds. Competitions are organized by age so you can test your skill and ability among your peers.

United States Masters Swimming, Inc.
National Office
2 Peters Avenue
Rutland, MA 01543
(508) 866-6631

AQUA DYNAMICS

The President's Council on Physical Fitness and Sports has designed a program of strength, flexibility, and endurance exercises that can be performed in any swimming facility. Write for their booklet "Aqua Dynamics," S/N 040-000-00360-6.

The Superintendent of Documents
Government Printing Office
Washington, DC 20402-9325
(202) 783-3238

TAI CHI CHUAN

Tai Chi Chuan is an ancient Chinese martial art based on universal principles of body mechanics. It is practiced more as a means of defending oneself from the internal enemy of stress than from external enemies. Its slow, gentle movements lubricate the body, improving blood circulation, calming nerves, and preventing illness. Practiced by thousands of Chinese, Tai Chi Chuan is especially beneficial to our high-stress culture. Tai Chi is easy to learn, and it takes only ten minutes to complete the entire form. Anyone who can move slowly can obtain benefits from its smooth, continuous movements, which focus the mind and calm the nerves.

Tai Chi Chuan is taught at schools, YMCAs, and similar organizations throughout the world. Master William C. C. Chen offers workshops across the country. For a schedule contact:

William C. C. Chen
725 Sixth Avenue
New York, NY 10010
(212) 675-2616

NATIONAL ORGANIZATIONS AND EVENTS

NATIONAL SENIOR SPORTS ASSOCIATION (NASSA)

The National Senior Sports Association organizes recreational and competitive events in golf, tennis, and bowling at some of the world's premier resorts. Members are all over fifty. While most are married, singles are also welcome, and many have found their "love match" at NASSA events. People of all skill levels, including beginners, are welcome. Those who don't play sports can enjoy many other activities, such as local attractions and shopping excursions.

NASSA is able to provide excellent first-class packages at affordable prices by using group purchasing power and scheduling during slower seasons. Bowling events are held at such places as Las Vegas, Reno, and Atlantic City. Golf and tennis outings follow the sun: In winter they are held in the Caribbean, Hawaii, Florida, or California. In the summer, they are held in Michigan, Oregon, or Canada.

Members of NASSA receive many other benefits, such as discounts on car rentals and sports apparel. The monthly newsletter, "Senior Sports News," keeps members up-to-date on outings, members' achievements, and other news and features of interest.

National Senior Sports Association
Suite 205
10560 Main Street
Fairfax, VA 22030
(703) 385-7540

US NATIONAL SENIOR SPORTS CLASSIC— THE SENIOR OLYMPICS

The US National Senior Sports Classic is held every two years in a different host city. Participants must be at least age fifty-five and place first, second, or third in their age group at local senior games sanctioned as a qualifying site by USNSO. Sports categories range from archery and badminton to swimming, cycling, and track and field. Less strenuous sports such as horseshoes, shuffleboard, golf, and softball are included.

Phil Mulkey, who participated in the 1960 Olympics in Rome, now competes in the Senior Olympics. At fifty-six, he is considered one of the babies. He won the gold medal for the high jump at the last Senior Olympics, breaking the record for his age group. "I still feel the competitive fires. My heart was beating out of my jersey because I wanted to do my best. If it were not for games like this, I might let down. I wouldn't be fit. Without Senior Olympics I'd still train, but with no place to put it to a competitive test." Eighty-four-year-old William E. Maine won several gold medals at the last Senior Olympics. "When I go out for events, I run as fast as I can," he said. "I don't run like some doddering eighty- or ninety-year-old man. I'll start playing golf when I'm one hundred, because right now that's too tame for me (*Sports Illustrated*, July 3, 1989).

US National Senior Sports Organization
Suite N300
14323 South Outer Forty Road
Chesterfield, MO 63017
(314) 878-4900

NATIONAL HANDICAPPED SPORTS

National Handicapped Sports promotes the participation of disabled people in sports and fitness activities. Through a network of sixty chapters nationwide, it conducts such activities as camping, hiking, biking, horseback riding, water skiing, ten-kilometer runs, white-water rafting, mountain climbing, and snow skiing. Members receive "Handicapped Sports Report," keeping them up-to-date on competitions, events, and outstanding disabled athletes.

National Handicapped Sports
Suite 717
1145 19th Street NW
Washington, DC 20036
(301) 652-7505
TDD for hearing impaired:
(301) 652-0119

WORLD SENIOR GAMES

The World Senior Games have been held in Saint George, Utah, every year since 1987. The 1990 games attracted 1,080 participants from forty-one states, Canada, Germany, and Mexico. Events include tennis, golf, horseshoes, cycling, road racing, basketball, softball, swimming, and table tennis.

Huntsman Chemical's World Senior Games
1355 South Foothill Drive
Salt Lake City, UT 84108
(800) 562-1268

PUBLICATIONS

The following publications can provide you with further information on exercise and fitness:

Your local heart association will give you copies of their free booklets "E is for Exercise" and "Exercise and Your Heart," or you can order one from their headquarters.

American Heart Association
National Center
7320 Greenville Avenue
Dallas, TX 75231
(214) 373-6300

Several books of interest can be found in your local library, bookstore, or can be ordered from the publishers. *Fitness after Fifty*, by Elaine LaLanne (Lexington, MA: Stephen Greene Press, 1986) is available in bookstores or from the distributor:

Viking Penguin
299 Murray Hill Parkway
West Rutherford, NJ 00773
(201) 387-0600

Pep Up Your Life: A Fitness Book for Seniors (Publication D549) can be ordered directly from the AARP.

American Association of Retired Persons
Fulfillment Center
601 E Street NW
Washington, DC 20049

CHAPTER VIII

Travel

"Afoot and light-hearted I take to the open road,
Healthy, free, the world before me,
The long brown path before me leading
    wherever I choose."

WALT WHITMAN
"Song of the Open Road"

At last you have the time to visit all the places you've ever dreamed of. You can go at your own pace for as long and as far as your finances will take you. Traveling involves more than the adventure and excitement of the trip itself. Planning beforehand and sharing your experiences with family and friends when you return are all part of the fun. Leaving the confines of home and exploring other places and cultures gives you a new perspective. You arrive home with a warehouse of impressions that linger long after your trip is over.

Though unpredictability is part of traveling, good planning can save a lot of aggravation and enhance the pleasure of your trip. Before going, find out all you can about your destination—its geography, history, and culture. You'll want to know about visas, passports, rate of exchange if you'll be traveling in a foreign country, how much you can expect to pay for things, climate, local customs, points of interest, and special events. Even if you don't stick to it, map out a route and decide how long you want to stay in each place. Maps of any country can be ordered from:

American Association of Geographers
1710 16th Street NW
Washington, DC 20009
(202) 234-1450

The American Automobile Association will help you map out the best driving route to any destination in the US. Investigate plane and bus fares. Shop around for bargains and discounts. Make transportation and hotel reservations well in advance and confirm them before you leave. Be prepared for the unexpected. No trip ever goes as planned or is fun all the time. Traveling can be tiring, uncomfortable, and scary at times.

There are many resources available to help you plan your trip. Libraries and bookstores have shelves of travel guides. Take your favorite guide with you so you can refer to it along the way. State offices of tourism and foreign tourist offices can provide you with lots of free maps, brochures, information booklets, and even information on transportation and accommodations. Travel magazines and newspapers are also valuable sources. Travel agents can provide expert advice free of charge since their commissions are paid by hotels and transportation companies. Some of your best tips can come from friends. You can learn a lot from their experiences.

If you're planning a trip within the United States, contact the office of tourism in the states you plan to visit well in advance. They will provide free information to help make your trip a pleasant one.

STATE OFFICES OF TOURISM

ALABAMA
Bureau of Tourism and Travel
532 S. Perry Street
Montgomery, AL 36104
(205) 261-4169
Toll free: (800) 392-8096
(In-State)
(800) 252-2262
(Out-of-State)

ALASKA
Alaska Division of Tourism
Pouch E-601
Juneau, AK 99811
(907) 465-2010

ARIZONA
Arizona Office of Tourism
1100 W. Washington
Phoenix, AZ 85007
(602) 542-8687

ARKANSAS
Department of Parks and
Tourism
One Capitol Mall
Little Rock, AR 72201
(501) 682-7777
Toll free: (800) 482-8999
(In-State)
(800) NATURAL
(Out-of-State)

CALIFORNIA
*(You may use either address
shown below)*
California Department of
Commerce
Office of Tourism
1121 L Street, Suite 103
Sacramento, CA 95814
Toll free: (800) 862-2543

California State Office
305 Hall of the States
444 N. Capitol Street, NW
Washington, DC 20001
(202) 347-6891

COLORADO
Colorado Tourism Board
1625 Broadway, Suite 1700
Denver, CO 80202
(303) 592-5410
Toll free: (800) 433-2656

CONNECTICUT
Connecticut Department of
Economic Development
210 Washington Street
Hartford, CT 06106
(203) 566-3977
Toll free: (800) 842-7492
(In-State)
(800) 282-6863
(Out-of-State)

DELAWARE
Delaware State Travel Service
PO Box 1401
99 Kings Highway
Dover, DE 19903
(302) 736-4271
Toll free: (800) 282-8667
      (*In-State*)
      (800) 441-8846
      (*Out-of-State*)

DISTRICT OF COLUMBIA
Washington, DC, Convention
  and Visitors Association
1575-I Street, NW, Suite 250
Washington, DC 20005
(202) 789-7000
Toll free: (800) 422-8644

FLORIDA
Department of Commerce
Visitor Inquiry
126 Van Buren Street
Tallahassee, FL 32301
(904) 487-1462

GEORGIA
Georgia Department of
  Industry and Trade
Tourism Office
PO Box 1776
Atlanta, GA 30301
(404) 656-3590
Toll free: (800) 847-4842

HAWAII
Hawaii Visitors Bureau
2270 Kalakaua Avenue,
  Suite 801
Honolulu, HI 96815
(808) 923-1811

IDAHO
Idaho Travel Council
Administrative Office, Division
  of Economics & Community
  Affairs
State Capitol Building
Boise, ID 83720
(208) 334-2470
Toll free: (800) 635-7820

ILLINOIS
Illinois Tourist Information
  Center
Department of Commerce
  and Community Affairs
310 S. Michigan Avenue
Suite 108, Ground Floor
Chicago, IL 60604
(312) 793-2094
Toll free: (800) 252-8978
      (*In-State*)
      (800) 637-5860
  (*If calling from Minnesota, Iowa, Missouri, Tennessee, Wisconsin, Kentucky, Ohio, Indiana, Michigan; all others call [312] 793-2094.*)

INDIANA
Tourism Development Division
Indiana Department of
  Commerce
One North Capitol, Suite 700
Indianapolis, IN 46204-2243
(317) 232-8860
Toll free: (800) 622-4464
  (In-State)
  (800) 289-6646
  (Out-of-State)

IOWA
Iowa Development
  Commission
Tourism Office
200 E. Grand Avenue
Des Moines, IA 50309
(515) 281-3251
Toll free: (800) 345-IOWA

KANSAS
Department of Economic
  Development
400 W. 8th Street, Suite 500
Topeka, KS 66603
(913) 296-2009
Toll free: (800) 252-6727

KENTUCKY
Kentucky Department of
  Travel Development
Tourism Cabinet
Capital Plaza Tower,
  22nd Floor

Frankfort, KY 40601
(502) 564-4930
Toll free: (800) 225-8747

LOUISIANA
Office of Tourism
Inquiry Section
PO Box 94291
Baton Rouge, LA 70804
(504) 342-8119
Toll free: (800) 334-8626

MAINE
Maine Tourism Info Services
The Main Publicity Bureau,
  Inc.
97 Winthrop Street
Hallowell, ME 04347
(207) 289-2423
Toll free: (800) 533-9595

MARYLAND
State of Maryland Office of
  Tourism
45 Calvert Street
Annapolis, MD 21401
(301) 974-3517
Toll free: (800) 543-1036

MASSACHUSETTS
Massachusetts Division of
  Tourism
Department of Commerce
  and Development

100 Cambridge Street, 13th Fl.
Boston, MA 02202
(617) 727-3201
Toll free: (800) 447-6277

MICHIGAN
Travel Bureau
Michigan Department of
  Commerce
PO Box 30226
Lansing, MI 48909
(517) 373-0670
Toll free: (800) 543-2937

MINNESOTA
Minnesota Tourism Division
Box 64215
375 Jackson Street
St. Paul, MN 55101
(612) 296-5029
Toll free: (800) 652-9747
        (*In-State*)
      (800) 657-3700
      (*Out-of-State*)

MISSISSIPPI
Mississippi Department of
  Economic Development
Division of Tourism
PO Box 849
Jackson, MS 39205
(601) 359-3414
Toll free: (800) 962-2346
        (*In-State*)
      (800) 647-2290
      (*Out-of-State*)

MISSOURI
Missouri Division of Tourism
Truman State Office Bldg.
PO Box 1055
Jefferson City, MO 65102
(314) 751-4133
Toll free: (800) 877-1234

MONTANA
Travel Montana
Department of Commerce
1424 Ninth Avenue
Helena, MT 59620
(406) 444-2654
Toll free: (800) 541-1447

NEBRASKA
Department of Economic
  Development
Division of Travel & Tourism
301 Centennial Mall South
PO Box 94666
Lincoln, NE 68509
(402) 471-3111
Toll free: (800) 742-7595
        (*In-State*)
      (800) 228-4307
      (*Out-of-State*)

NEVADA
Nevada Commission on
  Tourism
Capitol Complex
600 E. Williams, #207

Carson City, NV 89710
(702) 885-4322
Toll free: (800) 638-2328

NEW HAMPSHIRE
State of New Hampshire
Office of Vacation Travel
PO Box 856
Concord, NH 03301
(603) 271-2343

NEW JERSEY
Division of Travel and Tourism
Department of Commerce and
  Economic Development
CN 826
Trenton, NJ 08626
(609) 292-2470
Toll free: (800) 537-7397

NEW MEXICO
Economic Development &
  Tourism Department
Joe Montoya Building
1100 Saint Francis Drive
Santa Fe, NM 87503
(505) 827-0291
Toll free: (800) 545-2040

NEW YORK
New York State Department
  of Commerce
Division of Tourism
One Commerce Plaza

Albany, NY 12245
(518) 474-4116
Toll free: (800) 225-5697

NORTH CAROLINA
Division of Travel & Tourism
Department of Commerce
430 N. Salisbury Street
Raleigh, NC 27611
(919) 733-4171
Toll free: (800) 847-4862

NORTH DAKOTA
North Dakota Tourism
  Promotion
Capitol Grounds
Bismarck, ND 58505
(701) 224-2525
Toll free: (800) 472-2100
         (*In-State*)
         (800) 437-2077
         (*Out-of-State*)

OHIO
Department of Development
Office of Travel & Tourism
PO Box 1001
Columbus, OH 43216
(614) 462-4992
Toll free: (800) 282-5393

OKLAHOMA
Tourism & Recreation
  Department

500 Will Rogers Building
Oklahoma City, OK 73105
(405) 521-2409
Toll free: (800) 652-6552

OREGON
Oregon Economic
  Development Department
Tourism Division
595 Cottage Street, NE
Salem, OR 97310
(503) 378-3451
Toll free: (800) 233-3306
  (*In-State*)
  (800) 547-7842
  (*Out-of-State*)

PENNSYLVANIA
Division of Tourism
230 South Broad
  Street, 5th fl.
Philadelphia, PA
  19102
(717) 787-5453
Toll free: (800) 847-4872

RHODE ISLAND
Department of Economic
  Development
7 Jackson Walkway
Providence, RI 02903
(401) 277-2601
Toll free: (800) 556-2484

(*If calling from Maine to Virginia,
West Virginia & northern Ohio; all others
call [401] 277-2601.*)

SOUTH CAROLINA
South Carolina Division of
  Tourism
PO Box 71
Columbia, SC 29202
(803) 734-0135
Toll free: (800) 346-3634

SOUTH DAKOTA
South Dakota Tourism
Capital Lake Plaza
Box 6000, Room 623
Pierre, SD 57501
(605) 773-3301
Toll free: (800) 952-2217
  (*In-State*)
  (800) 843-1930
  (*Out-of-State*)

TENNESSEE
Tennessee Tourist
  Development
PO Box 23170
Nashville, TN 37202
(615) 741-2158

TEXAS
Texas Tourist Development
  Agency
PO Box 12005
Austin, TX 78712

(512) 462-9191
Toll free: (800) 888-8839

UTAH
Utah Travel Council
Council Hall/Capitol Hill
Salt Lake City, UT 84114
(801) 538-1030

VERMONT
Agency of Development and
   Community Affairs
Travel Division
134 State Street
Montpelier, VT 05602
(802) 828-3236

VIRGINIA
Division of Tourism
202 N. Ninth Street
Suite 500
Richmond, VA 23219
(804) 786-2051
Toll free: (800) 248-4333

WASHINGTON
Department of Trade and
   Economic Development
Tourism Development Division
101 General Administration
   Building
Olympia, WA 98504
(206) 753-5600
Toll free: (800) 544-1800

WEST VIRGINIA
Department of Commerce
Tourism Division
State Capitol
Charleston, WV 25305
(304) 348-2766
Toll free: (800) 225-5982

WISCONSIN
Wisconsin Department of
   Development
Division of Tourism
PO Box 7606
Madison, WI 53707
(608) 266-2161
Toll free: (800) 432-8747

   (If calling from Wisconsin and bor-
dering states; all others call [608] 266-
2161.)

WYOMING
Wyoming Travel Commission
I-25 Etchepare Circle
Cheyenne, WY 82002
(307) 777-7777
Toll free: (800) 225-5996

If you need a passport, you should apply at least three months before your trip. If visas are required, apply even sooner because you'll need your passport to apply for your visa. To find out the requirements for the countries you'll be visiting, ask your travel agent, the embassy or consulate of the countries you'll be visiting, or the US Department of State at:

Office of Passport Services
Bureau of Consumer Affairs
US Department of State
1425 K Street NW
Washington, DC 20525
(202) 647-0518

Some countries require vaccinations. To find out requirements and US government recommendations, call the Center for Disease Control's travel information hotline at (404) 332-4559. (Their address is 1600 Clifton Road, Atlanta, GA 30333.) They can also tell you about recent disease outbreaks, potential diseases, traveler's diarrhea, and precautions to take with food and water. If vaccinations are necessary, get them at least six weeks in advance.

Review your health insurance policy before traveling. Medicare does not cover the cost of hospital or medical care outside the US, but some Medicare-supplement plans may. If your policy doesn't, it is strongly recommended that you get one that does. There are short-term policies designed specifically for travelers. You might also consider trip insurance to cover pre-paid expenses in case you have to cancel. Policies also exist to cover lost luggage or sports equipment. If you're planning to drive, check your automobile insurance before you leave to make sure it's been paid through the period you'll be traveling.

A good rule of thumb is to pack light. Nothing is worse than lugging heavy suitcases in and out of cars and through airports and hotel lobbies. Pack comfortable wash-and-wear items that can double for different occasions. You don't have to bring a three-month supply of shampoo. Toiletries can be purchased along the way as you need them. Make sure, however, that you take all the prescription medicine you may need. Take comfortable shoes. Sore and blistered feet can ruin any trip. A good pair of jogging or walking shoes will serve you well.

If you're serious about traveling light, consider backpacking. After retiring from a law practice, Manuel Schultz and his wife Nadine toured Europe with nothing but a ten-pound backpack each. Both seasoned travelers, they wished to avoid overloading themselves with luggage. Because they are long-time joggers and hikers, they knew they would enjoy such travel, but worried what impression they would make checking into luxury hotels "looking like old hippies." In fact, no one seemed to notice, and as they anticipated, they raced through customs, hotel check-ins, and even managed to run and catch another plane home after their return flight was canceled (*New York Times*, June 24, 1990).

Experienced travelers suggest taking a bag of essentials on the plane so you'll be comfortable even if you and your bags get separated. Include:

• medications
• daily toiletries
• a change of clothes

On auto trips, make sure you have jumper cables, a flash light, a first-aid kit, tire-repair equipment, radiator fluid, and an extra quart of oil, but never carry gas in the car. If you should get hit, it can ignite. It is also a good idea to have a towel, pre-moistened towelettes, water or juice, and snacks handy.

Never pack your tickets, traveler's checks, passport, or visa in your luggage. These items should remain on your person. It's a good idea to note the number of your tickets and traveler's checks. Photocopy the pages in your passport with your photograph, date and place of issue, and any visas of countries to be visited. If your passport is lost, take these photocopies to the United States embassy. They can usually issue you a new travel document in a few days. Mark every piece of luggage inside and out, and remove all baggage tags from prior trips.

To protect your property while you're away, take the following precautions. Notify the post office to stop mail deliveries or have your mail forwarded to a friend. Halt newspaper deliveries. Shut off the gas and water. Disconnect the phone. Remove flammable materials such as gas, oil, or paint. Ask someone you trust to check in on things from time to time.

If you should become ill or stranded, lose your money, passport, or luggage, or get separated from your companions, don't panic. There is help. In the United States and Canada, Travelers Aid maintains offices in bus and railroad stations and airports. In Europe, the US embassies are equipped to help. If an emergency should arise at home, your family can reach you by calling the US State Department's Citizen Emergency Center at (202) 647-5225. To help them locate you, register with the nearest US embassy in each country you visit. The Citizen Emergency Center also issues travel advisories on health risks in foreign countries. The center can be reached twenty-four hours a day at the above number.

There is nothing like coming home from a trip. The comfort of your own bed, home cooking, and a new change of clothes mean more to you than you'd expect. But returning to everyday life can also be a letdown. Plan ways to keep the flavor of your trip alive. Cook up the new recipes you learned for some friends and show off your photos. Before leaving for home, send yourself a postcard. You'll forget all about it until one day you'll open your mailbox and be flooded with memories of your adventure.

TRAVEL DISCOUNTS AND SAVINGS

Retirees can save from 10 to 50 percent on travel expenses on airlines, buses, trains, car rentals, hotels, restaurant meals, and tourist attractions. Minimum age requirements range from fifty to sixty-five and often extend to traveling companions of any age. Many times all you need to do to receive a discount is to ask, when registering or purchasing, if such discounts are provided. You may be required to show a membership card from a major senior organization, but often your driver's license or Medicare card will do. Always remember to ask before paying anything. You'll be surprised how often you are entitled to savings. Other ways of saving on travel include taking advantage of off-season rates on transportation and hotels, "early bird specials" at restaurants, group travel, or package tours and charters.

The airlines offer many special rates. Most discount programs begin at age sixty-two, though some start as early as age fifty. Others require you to be sixty-five. Most will extend the same privileges to a traveling companion no matter what age. Various restrictions apply, such as day and time of travel. It may be necessary to make reservations well in advance to qualify. Several airlines offer coupon books or "passports" that are good for a certain number of flights within a designated time period. Check with each airline for particulars.

Both domestic and foreign rail companies offer substantial savings. A Eurailpass, providing savings on train travel within Europe, is available to all ages. It must be purchased before going overseas from the following address or your travel agent:

Rail Europe
226 Westchester Avenue
White Plains, NY 10004
(800) 345-1990

A European Rail Travel Senior Citizens Pass is obtainable in Europe. Individual European lines also offer savings.

Discounts are available on commercial, public, and sightseeing bus lines, as they are on car rentals. Many large hotel chains and restaurants have special rates, and some smaller, privately owned establishments do as well. Large attractions, such as Disneyland and Epcot Center provide discounts. Museums and tourist attractions also offer special rates.

Several organizations and clubs, such as the American Association of Retired Persons and the National Council of Senior Citizens, offer discounts, tours, and cruises to their members. The September Days Club, sponsored by Days Inn, provides travel discounts and services to its members. *Golden Years*, a bimonthly magazine published by September Days Club, focuses on travel and lifestyle issues. Mature Outlook Inc., formerly the National Association of Mature People, also offers discounts and a bimonthly magazine.

American Association of
  Retired Persons
Special Services Department
1909 K Street NW
Washington, DC 20049

The National Council of
  Senior Citizens
925 15th Street NW
Washington, DC 20005
(202) 347-8800

September Days Club
2751 Buford Highway NE
Atlanta, GA 30324
(800) 241-5050

Mature Outlook Inc.
1500 West Shore Drive
Arlington Heights, IL 60004
(800) 336-6300

Anyone under age sixty-two can save on admission and fees to the National Parks and historical sights by purchasing a Golden Eagle Passport, which entitles the holder and a carload of accompanying passengers to free entrance at parks, monuments, and recreation areas administered by the federal government for a calendar year. The Golden Age Passport, a free lifetime entrance permit, is available to people sixty-two and older. Blind and disabled people may obtain a Golden Access Passport providing free lifetime entrance privileges.

National Park Service
US Department of the Interior
Room 1013
PO Box 37127
Washington, DC 20013-7127
(202) 208-4747

ACCOMMODATIONS

GUEST HOUSES, BED AND BREAKFASTS, AND SMALL INNS

There are many kinds of accommodations to consider besides hotels and motels. Guest houses, bed and breakfasts, and small inns are not only less expensive, but often more enjoyable than an impersonal hotel room. Many are historic sights furnished with beautiful antiques. The proprietors, in business for themselves, take pride in their establishments, and often include such charming touches as flowers or potpourri baskets in the rooms. They are also knowledgeable about the area and can give you expert advice on what to see and do. Home-cooked breakfasts with fresh breads, muffins, and local delicacies can be wonderful. They may have libraries filled with interesting volumes to pass the time or a fireplace to warm you at the end of the day. It's generally easier to meet people and make friends in such cozy environments. Hotels never match the authentic flavor of such places.

You'll find many guidebooks detailing guest houses, bed and breakfasts, and small inns. Look in the travel sections of newspapers or in travel magazines for advertisements. The local chamber of commerce of the area you wish to visit can also help you locate such places.

YOUTH HOSTELS

Don't let the name fool you. Most youth hostels are open to people of all ages. They provide simple accommodations, usually dormitory-style with separate quarters for men and women. You can request a lower bunk if access or fear of heights is a problem. Many also have rooms for families or couples that can be reserved in advance. Most provide self-service kitchens equipped with pots, pans, dishes, and utensils. You bring your own food, sleeping sack (a sheet sewn into a sack), and towels.

You'll find hostels located in gateway cities, national parks, and near local and natural attractions throughout the United States and Europe. Some are housed in beautiful, historic buildings allowing firsthand appreciation of these sites. Reservations are not required, though they are recommended during peak season. You'll need to show your membership card and sleeping sack and pay a small fee.

Membership in American Youth Hostels entitles you to more than overnight accommodations. You also receive the American Youth Hostels Handbook, providing detailed information on more than 200 hostels in the US; *Knapsack Magazine*, filled with helpful hints for hostelers; and "AYH Council Newsletter," with information on events, activities, and trips. Members are also entitled to discounts on travel equipment, car rentals, and admissions.

American Youth Hostels, Inc.
PO Box 37613
Washington, DC 20013-7613
(202) 783-6161

HOME SWAPPING

What could be more comfortable than a home away from home? If you prefer a living room to a lobby and your own cooking to restaurant food, consider renting someone's home, condominium, or apartment, or swapping yours for theirs. You can get listings of such possibilities from the local chamber of commerce. There are also brokers who can help you find places in the US and Europe. Their fees are based on length of stay.

Intervac US
PO Box 190070
San Francisco, CA 94119
(415) 435-3497

Better Homes and Travel
Suite 14D
PO Box 268
185 Park Row
New York, NY 10038
(212) 349-5340

Vacation Exchange Club
Unit 12
12006 111th Avenue
Youngstown, AZ 85363
(602) 972-2186

If you are a retired or active teacher of any sort, contact:

Teacher Swap
PO Box 4130
Rocky Point, NY 11778
(516) 744-6403

TRAVEL COMPANIONS

Many people prefer to travel with others instead of alone. They enjoy having someone to share their experiences with and feel safer with someone else around. It is also less expensive to travel with a companion, and the travel industry is couple-oriented: Most prices are based on double occupancy, and singles are usually charged a singles supplement, which adds a lot to the bill.

If you find yourself without a travel companion, you don't have to give up your dreams of travel. There are lots of people like you, and companies make a business of getting you together. You tell them who you are, what your likes and dislikes are, the type of travel partner you're looking for, and they'll arrange a meeting. They also offer trips, get-togethers, and newsletters.

For more information, contact:

Travel Companion Exchange, Inc.
PO Box 833
Amityville, NY 11701
(516) 454-0880

Golden Companions
PO Box 754
Pullman, WA 99163
(509) 334-9351

RECREATIONAL VEHICLES (RV)

The term "RV" applies to any vehicle with sleeping space for camping out. RVs are the travel and lifestyle choice of many retired Americans. The freedom to pick up at a moment's notice or stay as long as you want is one of the advantages. It is also economical, costing about a third or less than staying in motels and eating in restaurants. The average fee for staying in a commercial camp is quite low and it is even possible to find places to camp for free. Cooking your own meals not only saves on expenses, but also lets you tend to any specific dietary needs you may have. This does not mean you have to rough it. Life in a trailer camp can be quite luxurious. Not only do they supply water, electricity, and sanitary services, but many also offer laundry facilities, stores, and snack bars as well as a host of recreational facilities such as swimming pools, boat docks, riding stables, and game rooms. The most posh even provide hot tubs, health clubs, and tennis courts.

Though economics and freedom are major advantages of RV travel, enthusiasts cite companionship as their greatest incentive. They can pull up to any campsite in the country and find an instant circle of friends. RV campers are like a nomadic tribe whose members feel a kinship with each other, though the individuals may be total strangers. Campsites are often abuzz with activities, from sports and game competitions to weenie roasts.

Several fraternal clubs enhance the camaraderie of RV travelers. The Good Sams Club is a network of more than 800,000 members sworn to come to the aid of fellow campers in distress. Members enjoy many services, including discounts, emergency assistance, campground directories, a trip-routing service, and a monthly magazine, *Highways*, that keeps them up-to-date on RV events and activities. Samborees and caravan tours bring members together for spirited events where they can play games, enjoy entertainment, and make new friends. With 2,200 local chapters, there is sure to be one near you.

The Good Sams Club
International Headquarters
PO Box 500
Agoura CA 91301
(818) 991-4980

Holiday Ramblers Vehicle Club is open to owners of recreational vehicles manufactured by the Holiday Rambler

Corporation. Year-round programs include national, regional, and state rallies, weekend campouts, and caravan tours. Their club newspaper, *Holiday Ramblings*, keeps members informed of group activities.

Holiday Ramblers
PO Box 587
400 Indiana Avenue
Wakarusa, IN 46573
(219) 862-7330

Single campers need never feel alone. Loners on Wheels invites you to travel and camp with them. You'll find other mature singles across the US and Canada to eat with, play with, and get to know. National rallies, campouts, and local chapters provide plenty of activities. A typical rally includes games, sports, music, dancing, and campfires. A monthly newsletter keeps you informed of events and in touch with fellow Loners.

Loners on Wheels, Inc.
PO Box 1355
Poplar Bluff, MO 63901

TOURS

There are many reasons you might consider a package tour instead of independent travel. Most tour companies are in business to assure you a comfortable, safe, enjoyable trip and are experienced in the type of travel you want to do. You can leave the scheduling, reservation-making, and other details to them. Because of the buying power of a group, the rates you pay should be lower. Also, there is safety in numbers. You might feel more comfortable venturing into strange places with a group of people than you would on your own. Taking a tour, you'll be assured of plenty of traveling companions.

There are all sorts of tours to choose from: adventure tours, learning tours, sightseeing tours, and specialized tours for specific interests or needs. The following is a brief selection of some of the tours available.

SAGA HOLIDAYS

Saga Holidays has been in the business of running tours for older adults for forty years. They offer a large selection of exciting, active, and educational tours all over the world. Most are value-priced and every tour is escorted by members of Saga's knowledgeable staff. You may travel by coach, take a cruise, or stay in one location until you get to know it. Saga can take you on an African safari or on tours of the Swiss Alps, the Great Smoky Mountains, or great gardens of the East Coast.

Saga Holidays
Saga International, Ltd.
120 Boylston Street
Boston, MA 02116-9719
(800) 343-0273

LAZYBONES TOURS

Some people avoid tours because they don't like to wake at dawn to be hustled in and out of a bus all day. They like to take their time and enjoy things at a comfortable pace. Those are the people Lazybones Tours are designed for. Lazybones Tours believes in restful vacations. They can take you on a leisurely tour of Ireland, Russia, or the Canadian Rockies.

Lazybones Tours
Evergreen Travel Service, Inc.
Suite 13
4114-198th SW
Lynnwood, WA 98036-6742
(800) 435-2288

AARP TRAVEL EXPERIENCE FROM AMERICAN EXPRESS

Members of the American Association of Retired Persons can enjoy the benefits of the special group-travel service from American Express. They can choose from a variety of programs designed especially for them, including escorted tours, discount cruises, hosted apartments abroad, fly-drive programs, and city-stay packages. Traveling with other AARP members insures companionship with those of like interests. Arrangements can be made through American Express travel offices, your local travel agent, or by calling the AARP Travel Experience toll-free number, (800) 927-0111. Cruise programs can be booked by calling (800) 745-4567. For information, contact:

AARP Travel Experience from
   American Express
PO Box 37580
Louisville, KY 40233-9895

GOLDEN AGE TRAVELERS CLUB

The Golden Age Travelers Club offers its members discount benefits, tour escorts, travel companion services, and personalized attention from GAT travel consultants. The *GAT Quarterly Travel Digest* is filled with all types of tours and cruises designed for the over-fifty traveler.

Golden Age Travelers Club
Pier 27, Port of San Francisco
The Embarcadero
San Francisco, CA 94111
(800) 258-8880

FLYING WHEELS TRAVEL, INC.

Flying Wheels Travel, Inc., designs group tours, cruises, and independent-travel experiences for disabled people and their travel companions. Escorted tours include such locations as Disneyworld, Yellowstone and Grand Teton National Parks, Europe, Israel, and East Africa. If you prefer independent travel, Flying Wheels Travel will help you design an itinerary to meet your specific needs and interests.

Flying Wheels Travel, Inc.
143 West Bridge
PO Box 382
Owatonna, MN 55060
(800) 535-6790

NATURE TOURS

Nature lovers will find an abundance of tours geared to the appreciation of nature. Many of these tours combine adventure and study with an emphasis on conserving our natural heritage. The following is a listing of some of the organizations sponsoring nature vacations.

Wilderness Southeast

Wilderness Southeast, a nonprofit school of the outdoors, invites you to leave the hassles of everyday life behind and allow the wonders of nature to inspire and teach you. Wilderness Southeast makes all arrangements for the trips, provides comfortable tents or cabins, food, safety equipment, and gear. Each day involves a leisurely exploration of nature with leaders pointing out interesting animals, plants, or natural events encountered along the trail. You may explore on your own or take advantage of your instructor's knowledge. Plenty of time is allowed for observation, rest, or photography. The evening campfire is a time to share the day's events and plan the next day's adventure. With Wilderness Southeast, you can explore such places as the Okefenokee Swamp, the Great Smoky Mountains, the Everglades, or a Bahamian coral reef.

Wilderness Southeast
711 Sandtown Road
Savannah, GA 31410
(912) 897-5108

The Audubon Society

The National Audubon Society sponsors more than twenty natural-history-oriented travel programs per year exploring the wonders of nature in such places as Alaska, Baja California, Costa Rica, Greece, Ireland, Scandinavia, and Turkey. All tours are led by Audubon senior-staff members who are experts in their fields. Bound by the National Audubon Society's travel ethic, all possible precautions are taken to minimize the visit's impact on the natural environment.

National Audubon Society
Travel Programs
950 Third Avenue
New York, NY 10022
(212) 546-9140

Harvard's Museum of Comparative Zoology

Take a safari to Africa, explore the exotic islands of the Indian Ocean, or climb the ancient Mayan pyramids at Tikal with Harvard's Museum of Comparative Zoology. Tours are led by top-notch naturalists whose expertise will make your trip an unforgettable educational adventure.

Museum of Comparative Zoology
Harvard University
23 Oxford Street
Cambridge, MA 02138
(617) 459-2463

Canadian Nature Tours

An appreciation of nature is the only requirement for joining Canadian Nature Tours. You can canoe the Kinogama River, watch for loons and great blue herons from a cozy houseboat, or hike through the Ottawa Valley wilderness. Tours are led by dedicated naturalists who volunteer their services. Proceeds from the trips are used to help conserve the environment.

Canadian Nature Tours
Federation of Ontario Naturalists
355 Lesmill Road
Don Mills, ONT M3B 2W8
(416) 444-8419

Wildlife Conservation International

The New York Zoological Society brings wildlife enthusiasts and conservation experts together to view the world's great wildlife spectacles. The program focuses on animals in regions of primary conservation concern such as: Rwanda's mountain gorillas, the animals of Alaska, the great wildlife spectacles of Kenya, the barrier reef of Belize, the penguins of Patagonia, whales off the coast of Baja California, and the unique fauna of the Galapagos Islands. Conservation experts and field scientists accompany travelers, explaining the biology of the species and the ecology of the habitats visited.

Wildlife Conservation International
New York Zoological Society
Bronx, NY 10460
(212) 220-6864

SEE THE USA

The United States is a fascinating country to explore; the diversity of travel options is sure to please any traveler and meet any budget. From the charm of a New England town to the bright lights of Broadway, from the grandeur of a redwood forest to the sounds of New Orleans, from the warmth of the Florida sun to the snowy mountains of Colorado, the USA provides an unending variety of sights and sounds.

Each state has an office of tourism that provides information on points of interest, special events, accommodations, transportation, and discounts. They also supply maps and guides. See pages 233-239 for a complete listing of state offices of tourism.

NATIONAL PARK SYSTEM

The National Park System, with more than 355 parks and monuments throughout the USA, offers visitors the opportunity to explore the great treasures of their heritage. From vast wildlife preserves to battlefields of the Civil War, the parks delight and charm campers, hikers, fishermen, hunters, sight-seers, naturalists, and historians.

The National Park Service provides information booklets, maps, and guides to the National Park System. For information, write:

United States Department of Interior
National Park Service
PO Box 37127
Washington, DC 20013-7127
(202) 208-4747

AMERICANA

Dude Ranches

City slickers with a hankering for the Old West can mosey on down to one of the many dude ranches scattered from Texas to Montana for a week of riding, roping, and general cow-poking. Cattle ranches have welcomed "dudes," as the folks back East are called, as paying guests since the days of Wild Bill Cody. Accommodations range from luxurious to rustic, authentic to newfangled. Most ranches are small, housing from twenty to fifty people in houses or cabins decorated in a western style, with touches like wagon-wheel headboards and blue-denim bedspreads. You probably won't find televisions or telephones in your room, but some ranches do have such modern conveniences as heated pools and hot tubs. Meals are usually served family-style and feature home-cooking and barbecue. Riding is the main activity, though you can get in lots of fishing and porch-sitting. Evening activities might include campfires, marshmallow roasts, and potato-sack races. The big-time comes on the weekends when rodeos and howdowns take place.

The Dude Ranchers Association publishes a yearly directory of close to one hundred ranches in ten different states.

The Dude Ranch Association
PO Box 471
LaPorte, CO 80535
(303) 493-7623

The following are three typical ranches:

The T Cross Ranch
PO Box 638
Dubois, WY 82513
(307) 455-2206

The Cherokee Park Ranch
PO Box 97
Livermore, CO 80568
(800) 628-0949

The Lazy Hills Guest Ranch
Box G
Ingram, TX 78025
(512) 367-5600

Wagons Ho!

Relive the adventure of crossing the prairie in a covered wagon. In early summer and autumn, you can join the Flint Hills Overland Wagon Train for an overnight trip through the only unplowed track of prairie left in the United States. You'll drink water from a tin cup, eat "son-of-a-gun stew" from a chuck wagon, and sleep under the stars. Though you won't have to reckon with any Indians or buffalo, life on the trail isn't exactly easy. You might face fierce winds, chiggers, or poison ivy and have to go on foot a bit when the wheels can't make it over a rocky hill. Then there's the relentless racket of the wheels and the jolting up and down over a monotonous landscape. The smell of fresh coffee brewed through a sock, the sight of flowers strewn through the prairie, and the sound of cowboy songs around the campfire are the simple joys you'll appreciate. You can even skip the campout and come back at the end of the day, an option not open to your ancestors.

Flint Hills Overland Wagon Train Trips
Box 1076
El Dorado, KS 67042
(316) 321-6300

Down on the Farm

Wake at dawn to the sound of a crowing rooster. Milk the cows. Then sit down to a huge breakfast of bacon, eggs, pancakes, sausage, fresh baked muffins, and strong coffee before heading out to the fields in the bright sunlight. Capture the experience of such a lifestyle by spending a few days at one of the many guest farms in the rural state of Vermont. Besides hanging out in the barn to feed and watch the animals, you can swim, fish, and watch the stars come out.

For a list of farm vacations, write:

Vermont Travel Division
Department R049
134 State Street
Montpelier, VT 05602
(802) 828-3236

The following are addresses of two typical farms:

Liberty Hill Farm
Rochester, VT 05767
(802) 767-3926

Rogers Dairy Farm
Rural Farm District No. 3
PO Box 57
West Glover, VT 05875
(802) 525-6777

PUBLICATIONS

The US Department of State Bureau of Consumer Affairs has prepared a free booklet, "Travel Tips for Older Americans," to help insure that you have a safe, healthy trip. It is available free of charge from:

US Department of State
Citizens Emergency Center
Room 4811
2201 C Street NW
Washington, DC 20520
(202) 647-5225

"Know Before You Go" details US customs regulations and duty rates. Free copies of this booklet are available at any local customs office, or by writing to:

Department of Treasury
US Customs Service
PO Box 7407
Washington, DC 20044
(202) 566-8195

Other government publications include:

"Your Trip Abroad," which provides information on passports, visas, and immunizations.

"A Safe Trip Abroad," which is helpful to people traveling in areas of high crime or terrorism.

"Tips for Americans Residing Abroad" is for those who plan extended stays or relocation abroad.

"Buyer Beware" lets you know what restrictions apply to importing wildlife.

To obtain these publications, contact:

Superintendent of Documents
US Government Printing Office
Washington DC 20402
(202) 783-3238

The International Health Guide for Senior Citizen Travelers, by W. Robert Lange, M.D. (Babylon, NY: Pilot Books, 1990), highlights what you need to know to have a healthy trip, including how to deal with specific health problems such as heart disease, high blood pressure, and diabetes; how to avoid jet lag and motion sickness; and what to do if you should become ill while traveling. Order a copy from:

Pilot Books
103 Cooper Street
Babylon, NY 11702
(516) 422-2225

Senior Citizen Travel Directory is compiled by Harry H. Henry a retired civil servant from Oakland, California. Harry began compiling various directories for older people when he realized how many resources were available, yet how uninformed people were about them. It has now become his retirement occupation, and though he does not seek credit or profit, he "gets a kick out of helping seniors stretch their modest income."

The directory is full of useful information, including contact sources for discounts on hotels, transportation, restaurants, and attractions. Various travel options are detailed, and a state-by-state listing includes campgrounds, RV parks, tour services, and points of interest. The book can be ordered directly from Harry Henry.

Senior Citizen Travel Directory
663 Carlston Avenue
Oakland, CA 94610
(415) 452-3167

The "Mature Traveler" is a monthly newsletter chock-full of information on bargains and trips. Special discounts are also available to subscribers.

Mature Traveler
PO Box 50820
Reno, NV 89513-9905
(702) 786-7419

The Senior Citizen's Guide to Budget Travel in the United States and Canada, by Paige Palmer (Babylon; NY: Pilot Books, 1991), is a handy little reference book that tells how to get discounts on all aspects of travel, including package tours and sightseeing information. It is available through the publisher.

Pilot Books
103 Cooper Street
Babylon, NY 11702
(516) 422-2225

Index

263

The author welcomes any comments you wish to share regarding the material presented in this book. Suggestions for resources to include in future editions and information on your favorite retirement activities would be appreciated.

Please address correspondence, including name and address, to:

Leisure Alternatives
42-15 81st Street
Elmhurst, NY 11373